THE FLYING SCOTSMAN

SPEED, STYLE, SERVICE

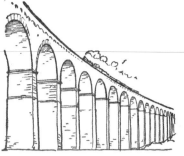
Royal Border Bridge

Durham Cathedral

Grantham Town Hall

EDINBURGH

MILES

$\frac{355\frac{1}{4}}{57\frac{1}{2}}$ *Berwick*

$\frac{268\frac{1}{4}}{124\frac{1}{2}}$ *Newcastle*

$\frac{254\frac{1}{4}}{138\frac{1}{2}}$ *Durham*

$\frac{232\frac{1}{4}}{160\frac{1}{2}}$ *Darlington*

$\frac{188}{204\frac{3}{4}}$ *York*

$\frac{156}{236\frac{3}{4}}$ *Doncaster*

$\frac{105\frac{1}{2}}{287\frac{1}{4}}$ *Grantham*

$\frac{76\frac{1}{4}}{316\frac{1}{2}}$ *Peterborough*

MILES

LONDON

$392\frac{3}{4}$

$392\frac{3}{4}$

Newcastle. Tyne Bridge

York Minster

Peterborough Cathedral

DONALD BLAKE

THE FLYING SCOTSMAN

SPEED
STYLE
SERVICE

ANDREW MCLEAN

National
Railway
Museum

SCALA

Produced exclusively for SCMG Enterprises Ltd by Scala Arts & Heritage Publishers Ltd.

This edition © Scala Arts & Heritage Publishers Ltd, 2016
Text © SCMG Enterprises, 2016

National Railway Museum logo © SCMG and designs © SCMG Enterprises

First published in 2016 by
Scala Arts & Heritage
Publishers Ltd
10 Lion Yard
Tremadoc Road
London SW4 7NQ, UK
www.scalapublishers.com

In association with the
National Railway Museum
Leeman Rd
York YO26 4XJ
www.nrm.org.uk

ISBN 978-1-78551-025-0

Edited by Jenny Lawson and Esme West
Designed by James Alexander
at Jade Design
Printed in Turkey

10 9 8 7 6 5 4 3 2 1

Every effort has been made to acknowledge correct copyright of images where applicable. Any errors or omissions are unintentional and should be notified to the Publisher, who will arrange for corrections to appear in any reprints.

Front cover: 'Take Me by The Flying Scotsman' LNER poster, 1932 (see page 116)
Back cover (from top): Workers putting up a 100mph restriction sign on the east-coast main line, 1964 (see page 50); 'A Smart Turn Out' LNER poster for The Flying Scotsman, 1935 (see page 117); BR lounge buffet car, 1951 (see page 77)
Front and back cover flaps: LNER luggage labels for The Flying Scotsman, c.1937 (see page 121)
Page 2: The Flying Scotsman window guide, 1962 (see page 26)
Page 52: Detail of LNER restaurant car uniform c.1930

Acknowledgements

I would like to thank a number of people who have helped and assisted with this book. I am very grateful to my colleague Bob Gwynne, my father Allan McLean and the Gresley Society's Chris Nettleton for sharing their immense expertise on the subject of the Flying Scotsman train, locomotive and route as well as railways in general. I thank them also for checking over the text and correcting many of my errors (those that remain are, of course, my own). Colleagues at the National Railway Museum have been extremely helpful, most notably Karen Baker, Amy Banks, Ed Bartholomew, Anthony Coulls, Tim Procter and Jamie Taylor with special thanks owed to John Clarke and Peter Heaton.

The National Railway Museum is part of the Science Museum Group, and I am also grateful for the assistance of colleagues from within the wider group, particularly Wendy Burford, Brian Liddy, Iain Logie Baird, Rebecca Smith and Michael Terwey. The book has been designed beautifully by James Alexander of Jade Design. Finally, the book has been edited with great skill by Esme West from Scala and Jenny Lawson from the Science Museum Group. A particular word of thanks is due to Jenny for her patience, professionalism and gentle cajoling to help meet particularly tight deadlines.

Andrew McLean

CONTENTS

INTRODUCTION

For over a century and a half a train service has run between the capital cities of England and Scotland. For much of that time this train departed at 10am each weekday from London's King's Cross to Edinburgh's Waverley Station. At exactly the same time another train departed in the opposite direction, and just north of York they would pass one another. From the first runs in June 1862 both trains were officially named 'The Special Scotch Express', but the popular nickname for the train would take over as its official title. That name is among the most famous of all trains: 'The Flying Scotsman'. A form of this train, which is the oldest continuously named express in the world, continues to this day.

'THE WORLD'S MOST FAMOUS TRAIN'

The story of The Flying Scotsman is one of competition. The rival railway companies that operated the two main alternative routes between London and Scotland – the east- and west-coast main lines – constantly strove to poach passengers from each other. They pushed each other to achieve ever faster speeds, even holding the much-publicised 'Railway Races' in the 1880s and 1890s. They consistently exploited the latest technological innovations to improve the passenger experience of rail travel, from early forms of air conditioning to on-board dining. And they developed publicity campaigns and brand identities that were streets ahead of marketing at that time. In its heyday of the 1920s and 1930s The Flying Scotsman, with its consistent branding and reputation for luxury, record breaking and speed, became an iconic symbol of Britain that attracted attention from across the world.

Opposite
1. LNER A1 Pacific locomotive 2563 William Whitelaw departing London's King's Cross Station pulling the 10am Flying Scotsman service to Edinburgh, *c.*1930. At this time the service was known as 'The Most Famous Train in the World'.

"Trains that pass in the day." *(Central Press.)*
THE UP AND DOWN "FLYING SCOTSMEN."

2. The two Flying Scotsman trains passing each another just north of York, *c.*1929. The simultaneous departure at 10am of trains from both Edinburgh and London was, with wartime exceptions, a feature of the service until being changed controversially in 1982.

It became the subject of music, books and film and built the foundations of the fame of the eponymous locomotive Flying Scotsman. It was known as 'The World's Most Famous Train', famed 'from China to Peru'.[1]

BEGINNINGS

The exact date on which The Flying Scotsman officially began has never been fully ascertained, other than to say it first ran in June 1862. It was Walter Leith, General Manager of the Great Northern Railway (GNR) in 1862, who first had the idea of creating the high-speed 'Special Scotch Express'. The train became known among railwaymen as the 'ten o'clock' but to the wider public as first 'The Flying Scotchman' and then 'The Flying Scotsman'. In July 1864 *The Oxford Times* explained to its readers the reason behind the name: 'from the rate at which it travels… [the train] is called the "Flying Scotchman"'.[2] The popularity of the service soon manifested itself in other ways: as early as the 1880s the train gave its name to the popular 'Flying Scotchman' pen, while in 1897

3. The stationmaster in his distinctive top hat dispatching The Flying Scotsman from Edinburgh's Waverley Station, 1936. For important services it was traditional for the stationmaster to personally see the train safely away. At the head of the train is an A4 Pacific locomotive Golden Eagle, in the traditional LNER apple-green livery.

4. The London-bound or 'Up' Flying Scotsman service preparing to depart Edinburgh's Waverley Station, 1936. The scene was captured by Dutch photographer Willem van de Poll, who travelled the world in the interwar years as a photojournalist, with a particular interest in transport, especially railways.

5. John Frederick Herring, *The Edinburgh and London Royal Mail*, 1838. Prior to the advent of the railways, mail coaches and passenger stagecoaches were the primary means of transport between the capitals of England and Scotland. Improvements to the roads in the first half of the 19th century did speed up the journey somewhat, but the coming of the railway revolutionised both passenger and mail traffic, with vastly improved speed and comfort.

the public was invited to a 'Unique exhibition' of 'Living Photographs' at the Regent Street Polytechnic in London including 'The Flying Scotchman at full speed'.[3] This was the first of many examples of the fame of the train permeating into popular culture.

From the beginning The Flying Scotsman service proved popular with passengers. Edinburgh was a major financial centre, and so the route was important for linking the Scottish capital to the London markets. The train also opened up Scotland as a tourist destination for the wealthy middle classes of the south of England, who were keen to see the land romanticised by Sir Walter Scott and popularised by Queen Victoria. But places along the route benefited too, notably the great industrial powerhouse of Newcastle and the

railway centre of York. As well as businessmen and tourists the train was popular among Lords, Members of Parliament, foreign diplomats and even royalty. But the train was also used by less wealthy second- and third-class passengers, not forgetting the modestly paid staff and crew who ran the service, including the engine crews (who became celebrities in their own right), chefs, waiting staff, attendants, guards and the men who maintained the infrastructure of the route. The Flying Scotsman was a train for all, rich and poor.

Prior to the advent of the steam locomotive, the only way to travel between the capitals of England and Scotland had been a 48-hour journey by stagecoach (fig. 5). This journey, which included numerous stops, was bumpy and uncomfortable, and, although the invention of macadamised roads did improve this somewhat, the smooth and fast journey that the railways brought was nothing short of revolutionary. The journey could now be completed in just 10 and a half hours, and that included a 20-minute lunch break in York. As early as 1875 *The Times* could report that 'The "Flying Scotsman" has indeed annihilated the space between London and the North, and the jaded citizen in search of health and recreation is transported in a few hours to the forests of Deeside or to the wilds of Loch Maree'.[4]

DEVELOPMENT

This reputation for speed was cemented and further advanced by the locomotives that pulled the train. Beautiful, fast engines were a hallmark of the line. The 'Singles', locomotives designed by Patrick Stirling, were introduced by the GNR from 1870. These were the first locomotive thoroughbreds and became part of railway folklore for their role in the 'Railway Races to the North' in 1888 (fig. 6). These races, where the operators of the east- and west-coast routes strove to beat

7. A dining car from The Flying Scotsman, c.1928. In the 1920s and 1930s fine dining, excellent wines and even, for a while, a 'Flying Scotsman' cocktail could be experienced aboard the service, all contributing to its perceived glamour and luxury.

one another on the run from London to Edinburgh, captured the public's imagination, and large crowds descended on Edinburgh's Waverley Station to witness the arrival of The Flying Scotsman. After one record-breaking run of 7 hours and 32 minutes a newspaper reported that people who had converged on the station were 'awe-stricken'[5] for 15 minutes after the train's arrival. So successful had the races been in raising the profile of Anglo-Scottish rail services that another series of races, this time with Aberdeen as the destination, were fought in 1895.

In the late 19th century second- and third-class passengers were admitted to the service. Although no longer the sole preserve of the wealthy, the extended service proved resoundingly popular. For many years it was common to run relief trains at departure times close to The Flying Scotsman's schedule in order to absorb the massive numbers of people who wished to use the service. With a reputation for speed cemented in the mind of travellers the train then moved on to develop its reputation for comfort. Brand new trains solely for use on the service became a regular feature from 1914 until 1948. These new trains attracted huge publicity: the modern rolling stock introduced in 1914, for example, was received enthusiastically. The new first-class restaurant car with its polished-teak partitions, green-tapestry upholstered seats, leather-topped tables and rose-coloured carpets attracted special attention. The consensus of those on board was, as the *Aberdeen Evening Express* noted, 'that no better or more comfortable travelling could be had anywhere'.[6]

Over the years this reputation was steadily built on as each new train improved in some way on the last: better heating, ventilation and lighting; more sumptuous interiors with improved soundproofing and double-glazed windows; enhanced facilities, including cocktail bars, hairdressing saloons and retiring rooms for ladies. But for all this, The Flying Scotsman remained an ordinary train open to all, one which offered, as one newspaper headline announced in 1924, the opportunity of 'Travelling De Luxe With No Extra Charge'.[7]

The 1920s saw the fame of the train rise to new heights. This was the period when the locomotive most closely

associated with the service was built: Flying Scotsman. Designed by the great engineer Sir Nigel Gresley and named after the train, the locomotive rolled out of the Doncaster works of the London & North Eastern Railway (LNER) in 1923. The LNER responded to, and also helped to drive, popular interest in the train and the locomotive through the production of related souvenirs, some of which became bestsellers. On just one Saturday during the British Empire Exhibition of 1924 where the locomotive was a star attraction the LNER stand sold some 1,800 postcards (costing 1*d.*) and 400 models (costing 6*d.*) depicting the locomotive.

The LNER kept the service in the spotlight in 1924 with the introduction of an all-new Flying Scotsman train pulled by Flying Scotsman and her sister engines, the fastest and most powerful locomotives in operation. The company also became masters of publicity in other ways: 1924 saw the introduction of Britain's first cinema carriages, which were attached to The Flying Scotsman (figs. 126, 127). There was also some tremendous good fortune for the Scotsman brand in this year. At the 1924 Paris Olympics a Scottish athlete

9. Photograph from the set of *The Flying Scotsman* film on the Hertford loop, 1928. The film is credited as being the first British talkie and starred both the Flying Scotsman locomotive and train. Here the film crew are seen setting up one of the many stunts that are a hallmark of the film. The other locomotive is K2 4668, which, like Flying Scotsman, was designed by Sir Nigel Gresley.

by the name of Eric Liddell won gold in the 400 metres final. Few newspapers passed up the opportunity to hail Liddell (later immortalised in the Oscar winning film *Chariots of Fire*) as the 'Flying Scotsman'.

Four years later, in May 1928, the first non-stop runs of The Flying Scotsman took place, becoming the longest regular non-stop railway service in the world. The train's reputation as 'The World's Most Famous Train' (a phrase used from the 1920s) was reflected by its role in two iconic films: *The Flying Scotsman* (1929), which was one of the first British 'talkies', and Alfred Hitchcock's *The 39 Steps* (1935) (figs. 9, 153–56). Although the 1930s saw newer, faster express train services such as The Silver Jubilee (1935) and Coronation (1937) take over as the east coast's flagship services, they did not survive into the Second World War, while The Flying Scotsman, by contrast, has endured in some form to the present day.

10. The Flying Scotsman, pulled by the A1 Pacific locomotive Merry Hampton, after its derailment, May 1926. During the General Strike miners deliberately derailed the southbound service by removing a section of rail near Cramlington, Northumberland.

THE FLYING SCOTSMAN STORY

The Flying Scotsman is more than just a train service. It is part of the story of Scotland and England, a piece of our shared social history. The train may have been famed for speed and luxury, but it has also seen its fair share of drama. It was involved in one of the worst accidents in British railway history when it crashed during a heavy snowstorm at Abbots Ripton near Huntingdon in 1876, resulting in the deaths of 13 passengers. In May 1926 the train was deliberately derailed by a band of hungry and desperate miners at Cramlington in Northumberland during the General Strike (fig. 10). By a strange coincidence the ill-fated locomotive pulling the derailed train that day – Merry Hampton – was also the locomotive that crashed at Goswick while pulling The Sunday Scotsman on 26 October 1947, killing 28. The Flying Scotsman was even a target of the German Luftwaffe in 1942, being shot at as it sped along the Berwickshire coast, although it is unclear whether the pilot was aware of the iconic nature of the train he was attacking.

But The Flying Scotsman has also been involved in other, happier, dramas, often on a personal level. A young couple who met aboard the first non-stop Flying Scotsman service from London to Edinburgh in 1928 became engaged three weeks later, married shortly afterwards and celebrated the 40th anniversary of their meeting by travelling on the special non-stop train hauled by the Flying Scotsman locomotive in 1968. There was even a baby born on board The Flying

11. A4 Pacific locomotive Sea Eagle pulling The Flying Scotsman near Burnmouth, Berwickshire, 1938. Burnmouth is on the stretch of the route that is dominated by spectacular coastal views. Three years after this photograph was taken the Luftwaffe shot at the train as it travelled this part of the route.

12. Silver commemorative cup, 1929. The cup was presented by the LNER to the mother who gave birth onboard The Flying Scotsman. The baby was named James Elner Scott, his middle name chosen in honour of the company on whose train he was born.

images in this book tell the story of this remarkable train, the route that it ran and the people that it served. They reveal both the 'hardware' of the train – the locomotives and the carriages that they pulled – and also the changing experience of travelling as a passenger on this great service. But the book also aims to showcase aspects of the train that reveal its place in the national consciousness, such as the 'spin-off' night-time sleeper version, the famous non-stop long-distance runs and the Scotsman brand that the LNER in particular so carefully crafted, and which has been crucial to the longevity of the service.

The book also explores the role of the train in promoting innovation and modern living through the use of the latest technologies on board, including radio, television and even cinema. The Flying Scotsman's reputation for speed was frequently utilised in publicity stunts, and the stories behind some of the most spectacular of these, the races against boats and planes, are also told. Finally, the book examines how the

Scotsman when Mrs Winifred Scott unexpectedly went into labour as the train sped southwards on 30 November (St Andrew's Day) 1929. A carriage compartment was pressed into service as a labour ward, and by extraordinarily good fortune there were both a doctor and a nurse on board. The baby was later christened James Elner Scott, his middle name in honour of the LNER itself. The company presented the baby with a silver commemorative cup (fig. 12), while his christening cake was modelled on The Flying Scotsman.

This book does not attempt to tell a comprehensive history of The Flying Scotsman but rather aims to pull out key themes and stories from its history, while making particular use of the objects and photographs held in the collection of the National Railway Museum in York. The

13. The Railway Queen Gracie Jones at Edinburgh's Waverley Station, 1934. The Railway Queen of Great Britain was a ceremonial position given to a daughter of a railway worker every year to promote the railways and British culture both at home and abroad. Here Jones is about to end a visit to the Scottish capital by boarding The Flying Scotsman accompanied by the sound of the bagpipes.

fame of the train was eventually subsumed by the celebrity of the locomotive that shared its name. The Flying Scotsman locomotive has come to symbolise nostalgia for a past – both real and imagined – when Britain led the world in many spheres, not least the high-speed luxury trains epitomised by The Flying Scotsman service itself.

TERMINOLOGY

To the uninitiated, railway terminology can be confusing. The most frequent mistake is to confuse a locomotive with a train (the latter is made up of a locomotive and carriages or wagons). This distinction becomes even more complex with The Flying Scotsman as the train is often confused with the locomotive of the same name. Indeed, The Flying Scotsman has, for most of its existence, been not one train but two with simultaneous departures from London and Edinburgh. In the 1920s and 1930s it was quite common for these trains to be pulled by locomotives other than Flying Scotsman, which itself was sometimes used to pull other services, meaning that there could, at times, be three Flying Scotsmen on the go at the same time! The LNER deliberately played on this confusion as they recognised the locomotive's potential to help promote the train.

The Flying Scotsman service has been operated by numerous railway companies. In its earliest days the train ran across the tracks of three companies: the Great Northern

Railway (GNR), the North Eastern Railway (NER) and the North British Railway (NBR). These companies operated the train collectively until 1923 when four large companies were created to run all of Britain's railways, including the London & North Eastern Railway (LNER) which took over The Flying Scotsman. With rail nationalisation in 1948 the service became the responsibility of British Railways (BR). Since rail privatisation in 1994 the train has been operated variously by the Great North Eastern Railway (GNER), National Express East Coast (NXEC), East Coast Trains (ECT) and, as of March 2015, Virgin Trains East Coast (VTEC).

The first locomotives to enhance the fame of The Flying Scotsman were 'Singles', so called because of their mighty single set of driving wheels, each wheel being 8 feet in diameter. There followed 'Atlantic' locomotives, named after similar American vehicles. Until the mid-1920s the train would change locomotive at set points en route, so each of the railway companies that ran the track of the Scotsman at that time had their own versions of the latest locomotive. When Flying Scotsman and her sister locomotives were built (1922–25) they were classified as 'A1 Pacifics'. The term Pacific refers to the particular wheel arrangement of the locomotive, in a formation of 4-6-2 with four small wheels at the front, six large driving wheels in the centre and two trailing wheels beneath the cab. After 1928 the original A1 design was improved to create a more powerful locomotive known as the A3. In time all the A1s were rebuilt as A3s, and Flying Scotsman was one of the last to be converted,

becoming an A3 in 1947. Among the later class of Pacifics to pull The Flying Scotsman were the celebrated A4s, the most famous example of which, Mallard, broke the world steam speed record in 1938, a record that stands to this day.

THE NATIONAL COLLECTION

The National Collection is the world's finest railway collection. It is housed at two principal sites – the National Railway Museum in York and Shildon, County Durham, both part of the Science Museum Group, the world's largest group of museums dedicated to science and technology. The collection ensures the preservation of cutting-edge technologies and strives to educate and inform the public about the huge impact railways have had, both in Britain and globally. The National Collection preserves a number of locomotives that at one time pulled The Flying Scotsman service: Stirling Single No.1; Ivatt Atlantics nos. 990 and 251; NER 1621; Flying Scotsman; the world's fastest steam locomotive, Mallard; D200, representative of the first class of diesel locomotive to pull the train; and Deltic King's Own Yorkshire Light Infantry, the most powerful locomotive operating in 1960s Britain. But the collection also goes beyond these 'star' locomotives to contain more day-to-day objects that reveal the experience of rail travel, including carriages, textiles, uniforms, models, toys, archives, photographs and books.

1   'Flying Scotsman The World's Most Famous Train' in *Portsmouth Evening News*, 21 September 1938, p.3.
2   Letter printed in *The Oxford Times*, 30 July 1864, p.8.
3   Advert for exhibition of 'Living Photographs' in *The Times*, 8 December 1897, p.1.
4   *The Times*, 16 September 1875, p.7.
5   'The Railway Race to Edinburgh' in *The Dundee Courier*, 15 August 1888, p.3.
6   'The "Flying Scotsman". Luxurious Railway Travelling' in the *Aberdeen Evening Express*, 4 July 1914, p.7.
7   'How Time Flies on the Flying Scotsman' in *The Arbroath Herald*, 3 October 1924, p.3.

18. The Foreman's hut at King's Cross station yard, September 1950. The Flying Scotsman headboard can be seen waiting for its next use. The board was attached to whichever locomotive pulled the train.

I. THE ROUTE

The east-coast main line, which connects London and Scotland, is one of the engineering triumphs of the Victorian railway age. The route is one of the most spectacular in Britain, taking in the sights of historic cities such as Peterborough, York and Durham, providing a vital link between the capital cities of England and Scotland, and helping to unite a kingdom. The first trains ran on parts of the route in the 1850s, and in 1862 the first so-called 'Special Scotch Express' ran the whole length of the line with simultaneous departures from London's King's Cross and Edinburgh's Waverley stations. This was the original name of The Flying Scotsman, which became the flagship service of the east-coast route, and captured the public's imagination in a way that the rival west-coast route (between London Euston and Glasgow Central) never quite managed to.

The east-coast line opened up the attractions of Scotland to new and large audiences who were eager to see a land popularised by the greatest novelist of the day, Sir Walter Scott. Scott was instrumental in creating the enduring romantic image of Scotland. It should therefore be no surprise that Edinburgh's major railway station, and the terminus of the northbound Flying Scotsman, is named Waverley, in honour of Scott's most successful historical novel, set during the Jacobite rising of 1745–46. It is in fact the only station in the world named after a book. Looking down on Waverley is George Meikle Kemp's Gothic monument to Scott, the largest statue in the world erected in honour of an author (fig. 31).

Queen Victoria and Prince Albert further cemented the romantic vision of Scotland by holidaying there frequently. The attractions of Victoria's northern kingdom and the popularity of The Flying Scotsman were captured by the artist George Earl in his 1893 painting *Going North* (fig. 20). It shows a group of fashionable passengers assembled on a platform at King's Cross Station ready to head north. They are gathered with their hunting dogs and sporting equipment, including fishing rods and golf clubs. The scene is set in August, the beginning of the grouse-shooting season.

The Flying Scotsman offered not only increased leisure and holiday opportunities but also speedy business travel between London and Edinburgh, the two largest financial centres in Queen Victoria's Empire. The east-coast main line became a vital artery for ensuring the growth and continued success of Britain and her vast Empire.

The Flying Scotsman's route along the east-coast railway also offered a mass audience – for the first time – the opportunity to appreciate properly the beauties of Britain's built and natural heritage. The journey afforded wonderful views of Peterborough Cathedral (resting place of Katherine of Aragon and original resting place of Mary Queen of Scots), York Minster and, surely the most spectacular railway view over any British town, Durham Castle and Cathedral (fig. 25). Other places of interest that travellers could see during the journey were Scrooby Manor House in Nottinghamshire, home to the Pilgrim Fathers, and the cottage at Killingworth, north of Newcastle, that was home to George Stephenson, 'the father of the railways'. Further north the silhouettes of Bamburgh Castle, the Farne Islands and Holy Island could be seen. Then, once over the Anglo-Scottish border, The Flying Scotsman would hug the spectacularly rugged coastline of Berwickshire before sweeping through East Lothian, with the volcanic outcrops of the Bass Rock, North Berwick Law and Traprain Law in sight, and on through the battle site of Pinkie, where the last major battle between England and Scotland was fought in 1545, before entering Edinburgh, with Arthur's Seat, Calton Hill and Edinburgh Castle providing a dramatic backdrop to the train's arrival into Waverley Station.

The LNER recognised that these views were an important part of passengers' experience of travelling on The Flying Scotsman. Passengers could buy window guides 'depicting and describing features of interest to be seen from the train',[1] and in 1928 the latest Flying Scotsman carriages were arranged to ensure that all compartment windows faced to the east, the side that afforded the majority of great views.

The route of The Flying Scotsman also changed the face of Britain itself. Some of the country's finest examples of industrial architecture were constructed as part of the route, the magnificent stations by Lewis Cubbitt at King's Cross (opened in 1852) and John Dobson at Newcastle (opened in 1850) being notable examples. Lengthy tunnels were also constructed through densely packed urban areas: travellers on the northbound train are plunged into the 'Gasworks' and 'Copenhagen' tunnels shortly after departing King's Cross. Great bridges were also constructed, including mighty viaducts at Welwyn (fig. 23), Durham and, most spectacularly, Robert Stephenson's High Level Bridge in Newcastle, which cost £500,000 to construct (fig. 26), and his Royal Border Bridge at Berwick-upon-Tweed, opened by Queen Victoria in 1850 (fig. 28). Later in the 19th century passengers travelling beyond Edinburgh on the northern-portion carriages that split from The Flying Scotsman proper would cross one of the greatest feats of Victorian railway engineering, the Forth Bridge, and the Tay Bridge, both the ill-fated original and its successor. It is unsurprising that the track of the Flying Scotsman was also known as the 'Great Bridges Route'.

The building of the Scotsman's route also had a major impact on Britain's built heritage, much of it negative. The ancient city walls of York were pierced to allow access to the town's new railway station. Trains including The Flying Scotsman had once reversed out of York Station until the new – and current – station was opened in 1877. Tragically, the castle at Berwick, scene of some of the most significant events in the history of both Scotland and England, was largely demolished to make way for Berwick's station. Similarly, the ancient Trinity Church in Edinburgh, which had been a place of worship for Scottish kings, was swept away to allow for the construction of Waverley Station. The east-coast route became a part of the British landscape, shaping the development of great cities and making dramatic interventions in the countryside. In spite of the losses that its construction required it was, and remains, one of the greatest railway routes in the world.

1 'From a Hotel Window', LNER advert, *The Times*, 10 May 1932, p.12.

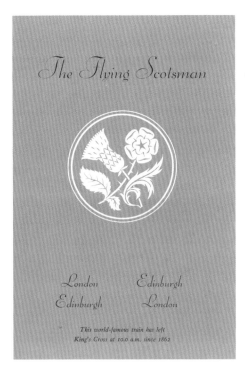

19. The Flying Scotsman window guide, 1962. BR produced this window guide, which points out interesting features along the route, to mark The Flying Scotsman's centenary in 1962. Along with engineering feats of the railway itself, many historical sites were passed, including York Minster and Peterborough Cathedral.

Above

20. George Earl, *Going North, King's Cross Station*, London, 1893. Earl's painting captures a bustling scene at King's Cross during the early years of The Flying Scotsman, with a group of fashionable passengers and their dogs, guns and sporting equipment, ready to catch a train to Scotland.

Right

21. Platform 10 at King's Cross Station, c.1928. By tradition The Flying Scotsman departed from this platform, but eventually the train had no fixed departure platform.

Above
23. *Welwyn Viaduct, Hertfordshire*, BR carriage print by S.R. Badmin, *c.*1950. The viaduct was opened by Queen Victoria in 1850 and is one of a number of impressive bridges on the track of The Flying Scotsman, often known as the 'Great Bridges Route'.

Right
24. GNER InterCity 125 or High Speed Train (HST) passing the line-side half-way marker between London and Edinburgh south of Tollerton, North Yorkshire, 2006. This sign was erected by the LNER in the 1930s and marks the approximate point where locomotive crews on the non-stop Flying Scotsman services would swap with the second crew. GNER took over The Flying Scotsman service in the 1990s and ran it until 2007.

Opposite
22. *Lines of Communication*, King's Cross, 1938, photograph by Cyril Herbert. This high-level view shows the railway tracks on the busy approach to King's Cross Station. The station is the southern terminus of the east-coast main line, serving Yorkshire, the north-east and Scotland.

25. Durham Cathedral seen from the cab of the passing A4 steam locomotive Dominion of Canada, 1957. In the foreground are Locomotive Inspector W. Connell and the driver Harry Willers. Although The Flying Scotsman rarely stopped at Durham, the superb views of the castle and cathedral from the train as it crossed over the railway viaduct were highlights of the route.

Right
26. Robert Stephenson's High Level Bridge above the River Tyne linking Newcastle and Gateshead, *c.*1895. The location of the bridge in relation to Newcastle Central Station meant that The Flying Scotsman had to reverse into Newcastle across this bridge until a new bridge, the King Edward Bridge, opened in 1906.

27. The 'Down' Flying Scotsman enters Newcastle Central Station, c.1930. Newcastle owed much to the railways, and the great railway engineering firm of Robert Stephenson & Co. was situated next to the station. Here the train is hauled by A1 Pacific William Whitelaw, named after the LNER chairman.

28. The Flying Scotsman on the Royal Border Bridge at Berwick-upon-Tweed, c.1937. The train is being pulled by A4 Pacific Golden Eagle. The bridge, which opened in 1850, crosses the River Tweed and is one of the masterpieces of the great railway engineer Robert Stephenson.

29. The sign marking the Anglo-Scottish border on the east-coast main line, 1952. The Flying Scotsman provided many points of interest for its passengers, and marker signs were erected at appropriate points of interest along the route. The original version of this sign was erected by the LNER in the 1930s.

30. Edinburgh's Waverley Station, July 1913. The
northern start and end point of the Flying Scotsman
service is dominated by both dramatic architecture and
landscape, including Arthur's Seat and Edinburgh Castle.
This view was taken from Calton Hill looking west over
the railway tracks.

31. A train departs Edinburgh's Waverley Station, 1934. The station sits in a valley between the old and new towns of Edinburgh. To the left is the Scott Monument, erected in honour of the great historical novelist and poet Sir Walter Scott. The station takes it name from Scott's novel, *Waverley* (published 1814).

32. LNER poster designed by Fred Taylor showing a view of the North British Hotel, Edinburgh, 1935. The hotel, designed by William Hamilton Beattie, was opened by NBR in 1902 and many Flying Scotsman passengers would stay in the hotel either before or after their journey.

EDINBURG

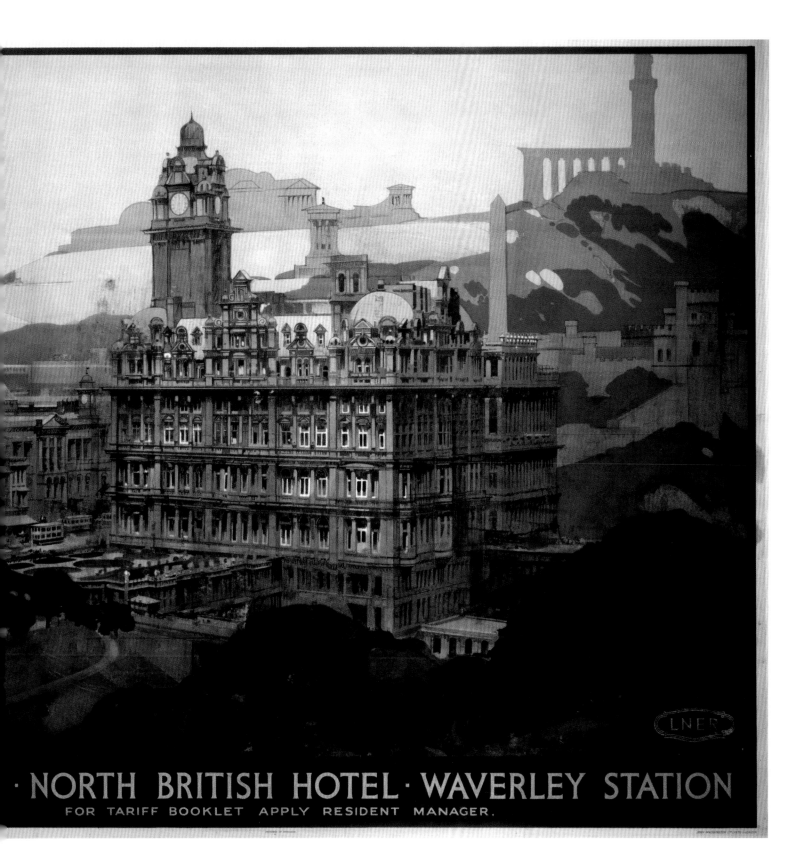

· NORTH BRITISH HOTEL · WAVERLEY STATION
FOR TARIFF BOOKLET APPLY RESIDENT MANAGER.

2. THE LOCOMOTIVES

In February 1923 a new express locomotive emerged from Doncaster Works. It was the first locomotive of the LNER, a company that had only come into being the previous month. The locomotive's designer was Herbert Nigel Gresley, the LNER's Chief Mechanical Engineer. As yet unnamed, it would go on to become the most famous steam locomotive in the country, its celebrity being built upon the fame of the train after which it took its name. It was, of course, Flying Scotsman.

The new locomotive was classified as an A1, among the most powerful type of express engines in the world at the time. Later prepared to a showroom finish in the LNER apple-green livery, with shining brass splashers and the company's new heraldic device on its cab, Flying Scotsman was to be one of the stars of the British Empire Exhibition held at the new Wembley Stadium in 1924 (fig. 112). The exhibition, the largest the world had ever seen, attracted an astonishing 27 million visitors and media attention from across the globe. The Flying Scotsman locomotive had become a media celebrity, a status that it would hold, on and off, for many years to come.

Flying Scotsman is only one of hundreds of locomotives that have pulled The Flying Scotsman service over the decades. Indeed the reputation of the service, which was already well established by the time Flying Scotsman rolled off the production line, was in no small measure built up by a succession of locomotives that earned the service its reputation for speed; these were the engines that put the 'flying' into the Scotsman service.

In the early days of The Flying Scotsman the route was operated jointly by three companies: the Great Northern Railway (GNR), the North Eastern Railway (NER) and the North British Railway (NBR). Frequent stops in journeys were thus necessary to change locomotive. GNR would run from London to York, with a change of engine also at Grantham. NER would take over from York to Edinburgh, changing locomotives at Newcastle and running from Berwick to Edinburgh over NBR tracks. NBR would later supply locomotives for this final portion of the route and would also haul The Scotsman's connecting services from Edinburgh to Glasgow, Perth, Dundee and Aberdeen. These companies, along with the LNER, who took over the route from 1923, built some of the most remarkable locomotives in British railway history to pull the Flying Scotsman and other east-coast expresses during the heyday of steam.

Beautiful, fast engines were to be a hallmark of the Scotsman route. This was epitomised by Patrick Stirling's 'Singles', which were introduced by GNR in 1870. The sight of these locomotives, with their 8-foot driving wheels and ability to pull staggering loads, captivated one young apprentice at the Doncaster Works where the locomotives had been built. His name was W.O. Bentley, and the beautiful cars that he would go on to design owe their inspiration to Stirling's locomotives.

Sadly, none of the NBR locomotives survive, but examples of some of the GNR locomotive types are now part of the National Collection, including Stirling Single No.1 (1870) and Henry Ivatt's small- and large-boilered Atlantics 990 and 251 (1898 and 1902 respectively). One NER locomotive also survives: 1621 (1893), designed by Wilson Worsdell. This was one of the locomotives used in the 'Railway Race' from London to Aberdeen in 1895, between the east- and west-coast railway companies, which attracted huge media and public interest.

The Flying Scotsman service proved so popular that more carriages were added to increase capacity, which in turn required more powerful engines to pull the service while still maintaining the speed that passengers had come to expect. The Atlantic locomotives were gradually replaced with Gresley's A1s, later developed into the improved A3 class; the Flying Scotsman locomotive itself was rebuilt as an A3 in 1947. Later came the A4 class, the most famous example of which, Mallard, broke the world speed record for a steam locomotive, touching 126mph in July 1938.

It was not unknown for Mallard to pull The Flying Scotsman service.

The feats of Gresley and his locomotives were cut short by the Second World War. Gresley died in 1941, and his beautiful A1, A3 and A4 classes became mainstays of the war effort. No longer immaculately presented, these thoroughbreds became workhorses, but they would emerge from the war to once more haul a number of prestigious services for the newly nationalised BR, including The Flying Scotsman.

From the mid-1950s BR were keen to modernise, however, and steam was no longer the most up-to-date technology. In 1958 The Flying Scotsman was pulled by a diesel locomotive for the first time, but these early diesel engines proved unreliable and it was not uncommon for a steam locomotive to take over. Indeed, the Flying Scotsman locomotive and her sister engines continued to be adapted to improve efficiency and performance. One of the most significant upgrades made to this last generation of steam locomotives was the replacement of the single chimney with a double 'Kylchap' chimney, allowing for freer steaming, particularly important given the great reduction in coal quality in the years after the Second World War. An undesirable side effect of these new chimneys was that the freer flowing smoke blew into the eyeline of the engine crew. To prevent this, smoke lifting deflectors were trialled on the locomotives that pulled The Flying Scotsman between London and Newcastle. Given a new lease of life by these upgrades, the A3s continued to occasionally haul the service into the 1960s, but by that time the service was dominated by the hugely powerful Deltic diesels, capable of sustained speeds of 100mph with heavy loads. The Deltic reduced journey times considerably and remained the preferred power in front of The Flying Scotsman train until the advent of the HST (also known as the InterCity 125) in 1978.

With the increasing standardisation of services, The Flying Scotsman was downgraded, but it enjoyed a renaissance in the era of privatisation. The Great North Eastern Railway (GNER) branded all of its trains with a logo that read: 'The Route of the Flying Scotsman'. One of these trains holds the record for the fastest journey time between London and Edinburgh (3 hours 29 minutes, set in 1991). They are powered by Class 91 locomotives, the first electric locomotives to haul The Flying Scotsman, one of which was renamed and branded 'Flying Scotsman' by East Coast, who operated the east-coast main line route from 2009 to 2015.

33. Postcard showing The Flying Scotsman, c.1880. The train is shown on the GNR section of the route near Hadley Wood, Greater London and is pulled by two locomotives, a Stirling 2-2-2 with 7-foot and 1-inch driving wheels and a Stirling Single with its larger 8-foot driving wheels.

"THE FLYING SCOTCHMAN", GREAT NORTHERN RLY.

The Knight Series, No. 599.

34. The Flying Scotsman in full steam, c.1895. Here GNR Stirling Single 663 is pulling a mixed train consisting of early GNR and later East Coast Joint Stock carriages. Prior to the creation of the LNER in 1923 the three companies that ran The Flying Scotsman built and owned a shared set of carriages to cover the whole journey under the East Coast Joint Stock name.

Above
35. The Flying Scotsman pulled by a pair of Worsdell NER locomotives in 1900. This rare photograph shows the train comprising of ECJS carriages at speed between York and Newcastle. The lead locomotive, 1629, was operated until 1945 when it was scrapped.

Left
36. Henry Ivatt's large-boilered GNR Atlantic locomotive 1442 pulling The Flying Scotsman, *c.*1910. The large-boilered Atlantics replaced the smaller-boilered versions – a reflection of the increasing popularity of The Flying Scotsman, which required larger and heavier trains and consequently more powerful engines to pull them.

Above
37. NBR Atlantic locomotive at Edinburgh's Waverley Station, *c*.1910. The Atlantic locomotives largely worked services north of Edinburgh but would occasionally haul Edinburgh to Newcastle services and were used on that route by the LNER until the early 1930s.

Right
38. A1 Pacific locomotive 1472, 1923. Soon after this photograph was taken the locomotive was named and renumbered 4472 Flying Scotsman after the famous train that it helped to pull. Sir Nigel Gresley's A1 Pacific class locomotives revolutionised express train services, allowing more carriages to be pulled while still maintaining the high speeds passangers had come to expect.

39. Gresley's LNER A1 Pacific class locomotive Donovan with Flying Scotsman headboard, 1928. Donovan was not part of The Flying Scotsman regular locomotive roster. It appears here to be filling in for a failed sister engine and has been fitted up with a borrowed corridor tender. Donovan's number was on its original tender, so the locomotive is shown here numberless.

Right
41. LNER locomotive 10000 at King's Cross with The Flying Scotsman, 31 July 1930. Known as the 'Hush-Hush', this was an experimental high-pressure compound steam locomotive designed by Nigel Gresley, who is seen here with drivers J. Gascoigne and R. Eltringham and firemen H.A. Brayson and J.W. Ritchie.

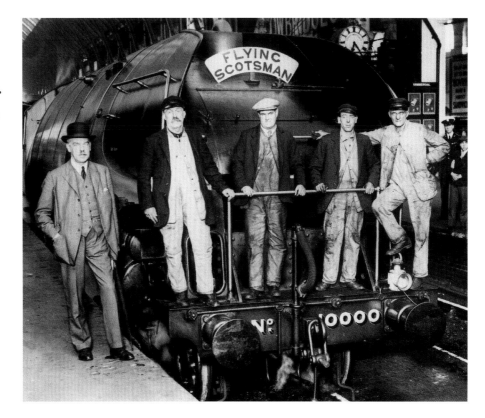

Right
42. BR A1 Pacific locomotive Bongrace pulling The Flying Scotsman, *c.*1950. By this time Gresley's original A1 Pacifics were being rebuilt as A3s so the 'A1' classification was now applied to these locomotives designed by A.H. Peppercorn, the first of which came into service in 1948.

Opposite
40. A4 Pacific class locomotive Silver King pulling The Flying Scotsman at Greenwood, New Barnet, *c.*1937. Silver King was originally painted silver-grey to work on another celebrated LNER express service, The Silver Jubilee. The locomotive was later painted garter-blue, the colour of her sister engine, the world-beating Mallard.

Left
43. Lineside sign between Hadley Wood and Potter's Bar announcing route modernisation of the east-coast main line, 1956. The modernisation of the route helped facilitate a reduction in the journey time of The Flying Scotsman and related services.

Below
44. Billboard at London's Liverpool Street Station advertising accelerated timings and new trains, 1957. As well as advertising the new Anglo-Scottish train named The Fair Maid, the adverts also announced the faster running of The Flying Scotsman by 37 minutes.

45. English Electric Type 4 locomotive (later class 40) at King's Cross Station, c.1958. This class was the first diesel to haul The Flying Scotsman. The early diesel services proved unreliable, and it was not uncommon for a steam locomotive to come to the rescue.

46. Attaching the golden winged-thistle Flying Scotsman headboard, King's Cross, 9 March 1964. The locomotive shown is Deltic D9010. The LNER had used wings to advertise the service as early as the 1920s, playing on the speed of the service. Railway staff and enthusiasts referred to this headboard as 'The Wings'.

Above
47. Inside the cab of a Deltic locomotive pulling The Flying Scotsman, 1964. The Deltics allowed for sustained 100mph running of The Flying Scotsman for the first time, dramatically cutting journey times.

Left
48. Workers putting up a 100mph restriction sign on the east-coast main line, June 1964. By the 1970s BR operated more trains on conventional tracks at 100mph or faster than any other railway company in the world.

Opposite above
49. HST or InterCity 125, 1981. These iconic trains took over The Flying Scotsman service in 1978 and owe much of their distinctive appearance to the work of the celebrated industrial designer Sir Kenneth Grange.

Opposite below
50. ECT class 91 Flying Scotsman, c.2012. This locomotive took the name Flying Scotsman when ECT re-launched The Flying Scotsman as a one-way service from Edinburgh to London in 2011.

3. ON BOARD

Although the service would go on to earn a reputation for comfort and innovation, travelling on the earliest Flying Scotsman train (or Special Scotch Express as it was then officially known) must have been a pretty grim experience at first. The small oil-lit first-class carriages (third class only being introduced in 1887) had 'good glass windows and cushions on the seat'[1] but no connecting vestibules, lavatories or heating (although foot warmers could be hired for a fee). Stops to change locomotives at places like Grantham allowed a brief respite, and a 20-minute lunch stop in York provided the sole opportunity for refreshment. But compared to the 48-hour stagecoach journeys they replaced, the early Anglo-Scottish expresses must still have seemed revolutionary.

It wasn't long before improvements began to be made to the passenger experience. In 1882 GNR started to install lavatories on its expresses, including the Scotsman route. Corridor carriages with connecting vestibules were added to The Flying Scotsman in 1898, and shortly afterwards dedicated dining cars were introduced as part of an all-new train launched in 1900. From then on new trains for the service would be introduced in 1914, 1924, 1928, 1938, 1948 and 1962, each showcasing the latest developments in passenger comfort and convenience: cooking by electricity, restaurant cars furnished in Louis XVI style, cocktail bars, on-board hairdressing saloons, ladies' retiring rooms, Vita-glass windows, which promised to be 'health giving' by allowing natural UV rays to filter through, and air conditioning were among the developments. In the words of Cecil J. Allen, the leading railway commentator of the age, these 'novelties' were 'designed to beguile in various ways, the hours of this lengthy journey'.[2]

By the 1930s the LNER's Flying Scotsman could proudly claim to be 'one of the world's luxury trains... an "Imperial Palace" in miniature, bringing London to Edinburgh and Edinburgh to London and weaving between them the even measure of a perfect service'[3] (fig. 56). Each area of the train was designed with meticulous care; the first- and third-class compartments and restaurant cars included unique designs for seat coverings, carpets, flooring and blinds. The renowned designer Sir Charles Allom was responsible for the decoration of the Louis XVI-style restaurant cars and the first-class carriages introduced in 1928 (figs. 65, 67). Allom was no stranger to fitting out luxury forms of transport, given that his firm also decorated ocean liners including the RMS *Queen Mary*. In July 1930 *The Times* reported that each first-class passenger on The Flying Scotsman would have a separate armchair, the angle of which could be adjusted.[4] Partitions in compartments were fitted with mirrors, and light was provided by 'Opal' electric lights controlled by passengers themselves. Heating and ventilation through the 'Thermo Reg' system provided a 'flow of warm or cold cleansed air... at the will of the passengers'.[5]

Such innovations had the desired effect of increasing the appeal of travelling on The Flying Scotsman. The LNER continued to experiment: the hairdressing saloon first trialled on the original non-stop runs of 1928 became – despite being lampooned in the satirical magazine *Punch* – a permanent feature until the Second World War (fig. 79). However other trials, such as the introduction of a cinema car in 1924 (see figs. 126, 127) and an on-board 'travelling bookstall' complete with newspapers, periodicals and books, met with varying degrees of success.

The dining services available on board their trains allowed the LNER to boast of 'modern hygiene, expert cuisine and swift silent service'[6] (one unfortunate bout of food poisoning aboard the train in the 1930s made no dent in the popularity of the service). Indeed the LNER would show off its kitchens and introduce VIPs to the on-board chefs (fig. 72). The chefs themselves were nothing if not resourceful, having to produce food for multiple sittings. On one occasion in 1932 it was reported that a cock pheasant smashed through one of the train's restaurant-car windows shortly after departure from Grantham, and that the unfortunate bird was handed to the chef for cooking.

One innovation that really caught the public's imagination was the introduction of a cocktail bar (figs. 76–78). The house speciality was the 'Flying Scotsman' cocktail, made from whisky, vermouth, Angostura bitters, sugar syrup and ice. The periodical *Railway Wonders of the World* said of the bar: 'This is a delightfully furnished room with ultra-modern decorations in green and silver, and the pleasantest of haunts in which to pass half an hour of the journey.'[7] For those not wishing (or able) to partake in such delights a buffet car was provided where, one LNER brochure promised younger travellers, orange and lemon squash was served.[8] The glamour and comfort of The Flying Scotsman in the 1920s and 1930s was not to everyone's taste: the poet John Betjeman commented in a radio broadcast in 1940 that 'Personally I don't like the new smart, jazz expresses with cocktail bars and heat which to me is stifling. I like an old, bumpy carriage with a single gaslight in the ceiling.'[9]

The austerities of the Second World War brought an end to this golden era of luxury travel, but a post-war attempt was made to recapture past glories with the re-introduction of restaurant cars on The Flying Scotsman. An all-new Scotsman train was introduced in 1948 complete with a buffet lounge car containing a 22-foot bar (fig. 83). There were further innovations: a buffet car with coffee machine, ice cream cabinet and automatic toaster, and in the compact kitchen the chef used the very latest catering equipment to provide the 200 luncheons and similar number of teas served on each trip. The quantities of food required to feed the passengers were huge: for example, after service each day the kitchen team would peel one hundred weight (approximately 50 kg) of potatoes ready for the next day's service.

When the latest Flying Scotsman train launched in 1962, some of the traditions of the service were continued but by now rail services were becoming increasingly standardised. Although the train now lacked the individual touches of previous decades (the ladies' retiring rooms had themselves been retired in the 1960s, for example) it was among the first to receive the latest and most up-to-date rolling stock such as the air-conditioned and double-glazed Mark 2 carriages (complete with public-address system) introduced in 1971. 'We shall', commented BR's Eastern Region which then ran the service, 'have the finest diesel hauled inter-city rail service in Europe'.[10] The launch of the HST (InterCity 125) in 1978 saw an end to compartment carriages on The Flying Scotsman, and the emphasis was now placed on bright, airy and open interiors. The HST restaurant cars still served excellent meals, and the buffet car had such novelties of the time as microwaveable burgers and draught keg beer on tap. For today's traveller there is little about The Flying Scotsman on-board experience that differentiates it from other east-coast expresses, a sign of the standardisation of railway travel but also how widely many of the innovations first trialled on this service have now spread.

1   *The Flying Scotsman: The World's Most Famous Train*, LNER, London, 1925, p.41.
2   Cecil J Allen, *Titled Trains of Great Britain*, 1st edition 1946, p.10
3   'The Flying Scotsman Non-stop', LNER advert, *The Times*, 22 July 1932, p.10.
4   'Flying Scotsman Innovations', *The Times*, 1 July 1930, p.18.
5   Ibid.
6   'To Scotland by day', LNER advert, *The Times*, 11 August 1931, p.14.
7   'The Flying Scotsman' in *Railway Wonders of the World*, part 6, 8 March 1935.
8   'The Flying Scotsman', LNER publicity brochure enclosed with 'Victory Flying Scotsman' jigsaw puzzle, 1936.
9   John Betjeman, 'Back to the Railway Carriage', BBC Home Service broadcast, 10 March 1940. Published in John Betjeman, *Trains and Buttered Toast*, John Murray, 2006, p.125.
10 'Air-conditioned trains for east coast', *The Times*, 11 January 1971, p.2.

Right
51. Edinburgh's Waverley Station, 1936. The bustle and excitement on the departing platform is evident as the 'Up' Flying Scotsman prepares for its journey to London.

Below
52. The 'Down' Flying Scotsman prior to departure from Kings Cross, 1962. This photograph is from a series on The Flying Scotsman taken by Cecil Beaton's former assistant John Drysdale, marking a century since the beginning of the service.

Below right
53. Refreshment seller at King's Cross Station, 18 December 1953. Once a common sight at major stations, refreshment sellers sold sweets, fruit and drinks to passengers before they boarded a train.

54. Actress and model Doreen Sinclair on board The Flying Scotsman, 1936. The Dutch photojournalist Willem van de Poll took various photographs of Sinclair aboard The Flying Scotsman in the 1930s. The carriage compartments shown in the photograph faced east, to maximise the best views of the journey.

Above
55. First-class compartment on The Flying Scotsman, 1938. Shortly before the Second World War the LNER introduced a new set of rolling stock for The Flying Scotsman.

Right
56. 'The Flying Scotsman Non-Stop' LNER advert in *The Times*, 22 July 1932. The advert indicates many of the attractions of travelling on the train: the Louis XVI restaurant, cocktail bar, ladies' retiring room and hairdressing saloon providing 'the even measure of a perfect service'. These all helped the LNER to boast that The Flying Scotsman was 'an "Imperial Palace" in miniature'.

The Flying Scotsman
NON-STOP

Louis XVI Restaurant

Cocktail Bar

Ladies' Retiring Room

Hairdressing Saloon

45 MINUTES OFF THE RUN

In the beginning The Flying Scotsman made its name by going fast, by running smoothly, and by arriving at the time appointed. It does more than that now. It is one of the world's luxury trains with *salon de coiffure*, ladies' retiring room, a Louis XVI restaurant, cocktail bar, "Vita" glass windows, and everything handsome about it. It is an "Imperial Palace" in miniature, bringing London to Edinburgh and Edinburgh to London and weaving between them the even measure of a perfect service.

The WORLD'S RECORD — 393 MILES

"The Flying Scotsman" runs non-stop between King's Cross and Edinburgh in 7 hours 30 minutes—45 minutes faster.

WEEKDAYS 10.0 a.m.
KING'S CROSS TO EDINBURGH
EDINBURGH (Waverley) TO KING'S CROSS

Ask for Pocket Time-table and Tourist programme at any LNER Station or Office, or of the Passenger Manager, Liverpool Street Station, E.C.2; or LNER, York.

KING'S CROSS FOR SCOTLAND

57. Selected material from a book of moquette samples for ceiling coverings, carpets and blinds, which was used to furnish the new Flying Scotsman train in 1938.

58. LNER fan decorated in the Chinese style, c.1930. Prior to air conditioning the LNER issued beautiful fans to help keep passengers cool aboard their services, including The Flying Scotsman.

THE FLYING SCOTSMAN
NON-STOP EACH WEEKDAY
LONDON AND EDINBURGH
(KING'S CROSS)   (WAVERLEY)

Air-conditioned Stock
Buffet Lounge   Ladies' Retiring Rooms

BRITISH RAILWAYS

PUBLISHED BY THE RAILWAY EXECUTIVE (EASTERN REGION) (A.D.804)   PRINTED IN GREAT BRITAIN   THE BAYNARD PRESS

Left
59. BR poster advertising air-conditioned carriages on the Flying Scotsman, *c.*1950. The poster, designed by Frank H. Mason, depicts the train at Edinburgh's Waverley Station headed by an A4 Pacific locomotive.

Opposite
60. BR Mark I carriage compartment, 1951. BR began to standardise carriages across all its services in the 1950s. This is a first-class compartment typical of that used on The Flying Scotsman at this period.

61–64. BR carriage prints, *c.*1949. Carriage prints were a feature of the compartments in the carriages of The Flying Scotsman at this time. These prints depict scenes from (clockwise from top left): Yorkshire Dales (Roland Hilder), Edinburgh (Edwin Byatt), Lincoln and Fountains Abbey (Fred Taylor).

Opposite above
65. Interior of a Flying Scotsman first-class restaurant car, 1928. The restaurant was fitted out in a decadent Louis XVI style to designs by Sir Charles Allom, whose firm also fitted out luxury ocean liners.

Oposite below
66. LNER triplet Flying Scotsman restaurant car set, 1928. Gresley designed the three-vehicle triplet restaurant and kitchen carriages with shared bogies, enabling smoother running, which was beneficial for food preparation and service, and passenger comfort. These triplet carriages were a feature on The Flying Scotsman during the interwar period.

Right
67–68. The Flying Scotsman's first- (top) and third- (below) class restaurant cars in use, c.1928. First-class passengers were seated on freestanding chairs. These publicity photographs were taken by the LNER to advertise the quality of service that passengers could expect aboard the train.

69. Christmas dinner being served on The Flying Scotsman, *c.*1930. Christmas dinner was served from early December in the run up to Christmas. Note the large plate of mince pies as well as the party hats made out of newspaper.

Right
72. Guests being shown the new all-electric kitchen car on The Flying Scotsman, 1928. The significance of the occasion was marked by the presence of high-profile guests Viscountess Elibank and Mrs Wilfred Ashley, wife of the Minister of Transport.

Below
73. Silver coffee pot engraved with the LNER logo, *c.*1925. Silver service was part of The Flying Scotsman experience for first-class passengers.

Opposite
71. Chef working on board The Flying Scotsman, 19 December 1933. The all-electric kitchens were much publicised for their modernity and safety, compared to earlier kitchens that had used gas. The electricity was generated by the coach's axles.

Left
74. LNER cathedral series dessert plate depicting York Minster by Wedgwood, 1930. The plates were introduced on the LNER's east-coast services, and passengers could buy souvenir sets to take home at the cost of 2s. a plate.

Below
75. LNER Keswick-ware dining service, c.1928. The thistle and the rose, national plants of Scotland and England, appear within the decoration, symbolic of the route of The Flying Scotsman.

76. Poster advertising The Flying Scotsman's cocktail bar by Maurice Beck, 1932. There was a cocktail bar on board The Flying Scotsman from 1932 until 1939, and the drinks it served included the specially created 'Flying Scotsman'. It epitomised the glamorous and decadent experience that passengers on The Flying Scotsman could enjoy.

Opposite
77. The cocktail bar on board The Flying Scotsman with corridor running alongside, *c.*1932. The cocktail bar was at the end of the carriage and, although compact, offered a taste of modern glamour and style.

Right
78. A couple enjoying a cocktail aboard The Flying Scotsman, *c.*1936. The cocktail bar was promoted as a 'pleasant' way to spend part of what was still a lengthy journey.

79. Doreen Sinclair having her hair styled on the Flying Scotsman, 1936. The hairdressing salon was run by B. Morris & Sons and must have involved extraordinary skill on the part of the barber as the train could reach speeds in excess of 80mph.

80. Miss Edith Patterson, Ladies' Attendant on The Flying Scotsman, 1929. Patterson was one of the attendants in the ladies' retiring room and was said to be 'the most restless woman in the world' due to her daily travels on the train, spending one night in London and the next in Edinburgh. Her nickname was 'the Flying Scotch Angel'.

Above
81. Waiter serving refreshments on the southbound Flying Scotsman, 1 October 1945. This photograph was taken on the first train to feature the reintroduced restaurant cars following their temporary abandonment during the Second World War.

Right
82. BR Mark 1 carriage kitchen car of the type used on The Flying Scotsman, 1951. Although restaurant-car services became increasingly standardised in the nationalised railways, the quality of cooking, equipment and service remained of the highest standard.

83. BR lounge buffet car, 1951. This bar carriage was part of a new set of carriages designed by Edward Thompson for The Flying Scotsman in 1948. The carriages were also used on another non-stop London–Edinburgh service, The Capitals Limited, shown here.

Above
84. First-class restaurant car typical of those on The Flying Scotsman and other BR express trains, 1955. Fine dining and expensive wines continued to be the highlight of the journey for many passengers.

Left
85. Waitress serving breakfast on an HST, *c.*1979. The HST was introduced to The Flying Scotsman service in 1978 and provided a fast air-conditioned office for business travellers along with meals served in a restaurant car.

86. Wine list from The Flying Scotsman centenary service, 1962. There were still a huge number of champagnes, wines, spirits, beers and liqueurs to choose from on the train at this time, including wines from France, Alsace, Spain, South Africa and Australia.

Wine List

The
FLYING SCOTSMAN
1862–1962

Robert Bartlett

4. THE NIGHT SCOTSMAN

To Scotland at night on the ten twenty-five,
The driver his vigil is keeping;
The passengers, knowing that this is the case,
Can lie in their berths sweetly sleeping.

LNER newspaper advertisement, 1928[1]

Such was the success of The Flying Scotsman service that in time derivations of it were introduced, including The Junior Scotsman, which was put on to cope with the additional demand during busy periods. There were also weekend versions and a sleeper service, too, the celebrated Night Scotsman. Just like its daytime equivalent, The Night Scotsman enjoyed the heyday of steam travel during the 1920s and 1930s, and it was run in competition with the rival west-coast London-to-Scotland sleeper known as The Night Scot, run by London, Midland & Scottish Railway (LMS).

There had been sleeping-car trains on the east-coast route from the late 1870s. These were composed of what one commentator called 'relatively crude'[2] vehicles. In the 1890s the three companies responsible for the east-coast route had introduced the transverse sleeping compartment layout, where the passenger lies perpendicular to the direction of travel, which has been the norm ever since. By 1914 the train departed King's Cross at 11.30pm every night, arriving in Edinburgh exactly 8 hours later. The length of the journey time would later increase, largely due to far heavier trains, so that in 1939, even with an earlier departure time of 10.25pm, the arrival time was 7.15am, making the journey 50 minutes longer on the eve of the Second World War than it had been on the eve of the First.

When the LNER took over the running of the east-coast route in 1923 they were keen to build upon the success of GNR's sleeper service, which last ran in 1922. As with The Flying Scotsman new carriages were introduced at regular intervals. These carriages were of the 'twin type', with two carriages being articulated or placed upon three bogies, the shared connecting bogie in the centre creating a smoother and more comfortable journey. Sleeping cars were no longer the preserve of the rich either, and third-class passengers were admitted from 1928 (fig. 93). In each third-class carriage there were seven compartments, each containing four berths, with lavatories and hot and cold water at the ends of each carriage. In first class there were ten single compartments each with one berth, a wash basin, hot and cold running water and steam heating. In the 1930s comfort was increased further through the provision of en-suite toilets and showers in first class.

The LNER recognised that they needed to market The Night Scotsman service as being both comfortable and safe. Some of the finest and most atmospheric railway advertising posters were created for the service, such as Alexandre Alexeieff's dreamy Art Deco poster of 1931 (fig. 89). Alexeieff was a Russian-born illustrator and innovative filmmaker of international standing who designed several posters for the LNER, and his 'Night Scotsman' design is now one of the most collectable of all railway posters with copies selling for prices in excess of £30,000. Continuing this high standard of advertising for the service, Robert Bartlett's visually stunning poster of 1932 advertised first- and third-class sleeping berths aboard The Night Scotsman, showing an A1 Pacific speeding into the night, the darkness pierced only by the fiery light of the locomotive's cab (fig. 90).

The Night Scotsman proved to be a huge success, and additional sleeper services were established by the LNER. By 1930, in addition to The Night Scotsman service there were also: The Highlandman, departing London at 7.25pm for Edinburgh then splitting with portions for Fort William, Perth and Inverness; The Aberdonian, heading to Edinburgh, Dundee, Aberdeen, Elgin and Lossiemouth at 7.40pm; an unnamed sleeper train for Edinburgh and Glasgow departing at 10.35pm; and, for those who wished to take in a show, a later After-Theatre sleeping- (first class only) and breakfast-car train, which departed at 1.10am and called at Edinburgh and then separated with portions calling at Glasgow, Dundee and Aberdeen, Perth and Inverness.

By the late 1930s The Night Scotsman had become so successful that it stopped taking reservations for passengers travelling to Edinburgh and became exclusively for passengers travelling beyond the Scottish capital. The train, which also picked up at Grantham, York and Newcastle, was split at Edinburgh Waverley, with portions heading to Glasgow, Perth or Aberdeen as part of breakfast-car trains. The displaced Edinburgh passengers were relegated to a service departing 10 minutes after The Night Scotsman. Strangely, it was only in 1939 that the equivalent southbound sleeper service was officially named The Night Scotsman, the name previously being reserved solely for the northbound train. As with the more celebrated daytime service, The Night Scotsman carried a headboard in Eric Gill's famous font in the 1930s (see chapter 6).

At the height of its popularity, in the years immediately before the Second World War, The Night Scotsman could be made up of as many as 14 carriages, making the train among the heaviest in Britain. As with the daytime Scotsman, the train was hauled by one of Gresley's powerful Pacific locomotives (usually an A1 or A3) as far as Edinburgh. The Night Scotsman was one of only four trains (along with The Flying Scotsman) to retain their name during the Second World War, but the name would later fall out of use for a short time before being revived in 1971 and used for the Edinburgh and Aberdeen train leaving London at 11.35pm.

The sleeping-car services from King's Cross heading up the east coast ceased in the mid-1980s, and today the only Anglo-Scottish sleeper services run between London Euston Station and Scotland via the west-coast main line. This service, known as The Caledonian Sleeper, was re-launched in 2015 and owes much to the standards set by The Night Scotsman, marketing itself on its comfort, facilities and freshly sourced Scottish food and drink. The service has ordered new sleeping carriages complete with en-suite cabins with showering facilities, a feature not seen on British sleeping cars since the glory days of The Night Scotsman in the 1930s.

1 'LNER Reminders', advert, *The Times*, 25 September 1928, p.16.
2 *The Flying Scotsman: The World's Most Famous Train*, LNER, 1925, p.54.

Right
87. Artwork of a night train pulled by a GNR Atlantic locomotive, *c.*1900. Sleeping cars were introduced on the east-coast main line in the 1870s and became so popular that a number of cross-border sleeping-car services, including The Night Scotsman, were introduced.

Below
88. ECJS sleeping carriage, 1906. The three companies that ran both The Flying Scotsman and The Night Scotsman before being amalgamated into the LNER in 1923 jointly built carriages under the ECJS banner.

89. Alexandre Alexeieff's Night Scotsman poster, 1931. Alexeieff was a noted artist, filmmaker and illustrator, and his involvement with the LNER demonstrates the company's famed forward-thinking approach to railway advertising at this time.

THE NIGHT SCOTSMAN
Leaves King's Cross nightly at 10.25.

PUBLISHED BY THE LONDON & NORTH EASTERN RAILWAY   PRINTED IN ENGLAND   WATERLOW & SONS LTD LONDON, DUNSTABLE & WATFORD.

90. 'Scotland by "The Night Scotsman"' LNER poster by Robert Bartlett, 1932. The poster advertises the first- and third-class sleepers available on the service, which departed King's Cross nightly at 10.25pm.

Overleaf
91. The Night Scotsman prepares for departure from King's Cross, *c.*1930. The locomotive is A1 Pacific Woolwinder, named after the winner of the 1907 St Leger horse race.

92. Shower in a new LNER first-class sleeping compartment, 1932. The shower was a new development as part of Gresley's drive to keep the LNER at the forefront of rail developments. The water was heated from the train's steam heating system.

Opposite
93. Interior of an LNER third-class sleeping car, 1928. This LNER publicity photograph shows how, with folding-down beds, a compartment could provide sleeping capacity for four people.

94. An LNER attendant showing a passenger into their sleeping-car compartment, 1935. On arrival into Edinburgh The Night Scotsman split into three component parts, which were added to breakfast-car trains for passengers travelling to Glasgow, Perth or Aberdeen. Those heading northwards could be tucking into a plate of kippers by the time the train was crossing the Forth Bridge.

95. The Night Scotsman's locomotive headboard as used in the 1950s. As with The Flying Scotsman, the headboard used Eric Gill's bespoke font. The board was affixed to the front of whichever locomotive was pulling the service.

96. Passengers prepare to board the Scotland-bound Night Scotsman, King's Cross Station, February 1961. The Night Scotsman was one of a series of sleeper trains between London and Scotland, some including stops in the north of England, enabling people to access London or Edinburgh for both business and pleasure.

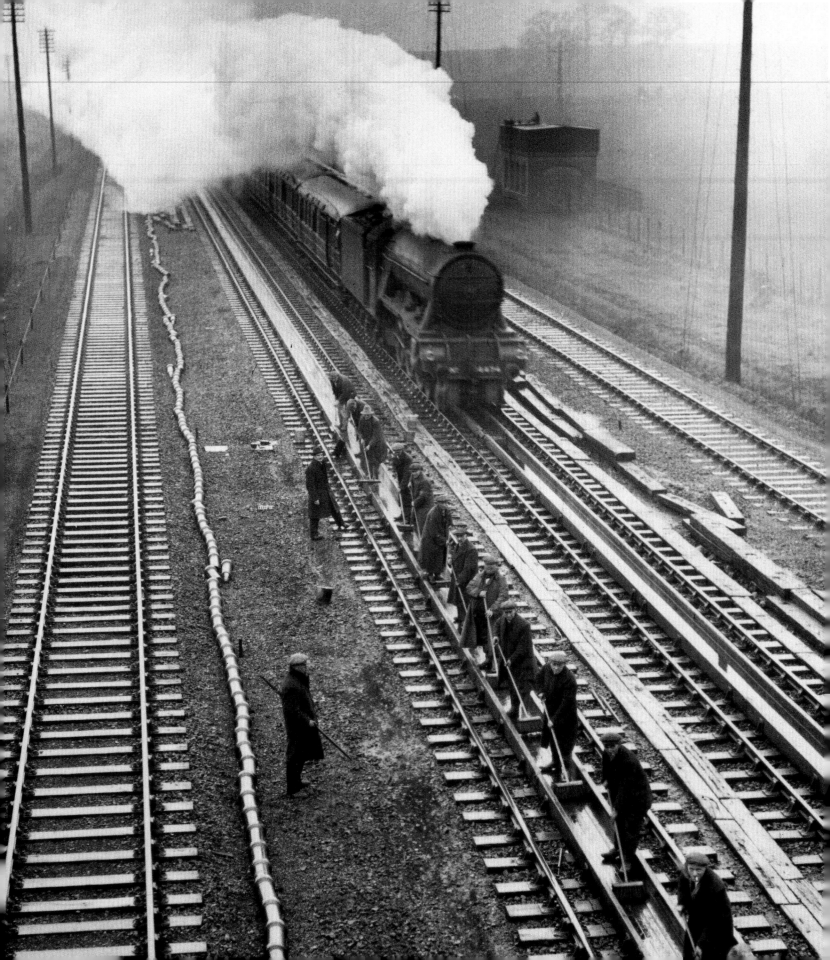

5. NON-STOP

On 1 May 1928 two trains named The Flying Scotsman departed London's King's Cross and Edinburgh's Waverley Station at 10am. This choreography had been the norm for many years, but on this day there was a key difference. For the first time the two services would complete the near 393-mile journey without stopping. It was a feat designed to secure the mantle of the world's longest non-stop railway service and increase the fame of the LNER's most prestigious train. But a few days earlier the LNER's great rival, LMS, operators of the west-coast route from London to Scotland, had got wind of the LNER's intentions and had run a longer non-stop train. All was not lost for the LNER and its publicity machine, however, as the LMS run was a one-off while The Flying Scotsman ran non-stop throughout the summer months of 1928–39, meaning it could claim to be world's longest regular non-stop train service.

The irony of this development was that – initially at least – non-stop runs didn't make the train journey any quicker, as the LNER was still bound by its increasingly ridiculous agreement with the LMS to run Anglo-Scottish expresses to minimum journey times that they were each capable of improving upon. This arrangement had been in place since the high-speed races between companies on the east- and west-coast routes in 1888 and 1895. Tied to this convention, the LNER sought other ways to enhance the appeal of The Flying Scotsman, and the non-stop runs attracted much positive publicity.

Large crowds turned out to witness the two inaugural runs, and the occasion was marked with much ceremony. At King's Cross the Edinburgh-bound train was seen off by Sir Charles Batho, Lord Mayor of London (fig. 99). The locomotive was A1 Pacific Flying Scotsman, crewed by driver Pibworth and fireman Goddard who gave way to driver Blades and fireman Morris at the halfway point. Meanwhile, at Edinburgh Waverley Station the southbound train was seen off by Bailie Hay, Senior Magistrate of Edinburgh, and his daughter who presented the crew of drivers Henderson and Day and firemen McKenzie and Gray with silver badges in the shape of Edinburgh's coat of arms with ribbons of black and white, the city colours. A horseshoe was affixed to the locomotive A3 Pacific Shotover. Both trains arrived to cheering crowds at their destinations.

Although the non-stop runs were restricted to the summer months and continued only for a few years, the publicity surrounding them added yet more prestige to the Scotsman service. The LNER took full advantage of this marketing capital, especially once the concord with the LMS not to cut journey times below 8 and a quarter hours was ripped up in 1931 and passengers could enjoy the full-speed benefits of the non-stop service. The company's publicity machine even suggested that the LNER acronym no longer stood for 'London & North Eastern Railway' but 'London Non-Stop Edinburgh Route'. By 1937 the journey – using the faster and more powerful A4 Pacifics – took just 7 hours.

The key development that made non-stop runs possible was the ability to change crew en route. It would have been impossible for one crew to run the train the full distance between Scotland and England. The strain that this would put on one driver, who would have to observe 700–800 signals, and on one fireman, who would have to shovel 8–9 tons of coal, would have been immense. Traditional locomotive arrangements would not allow for crews to be changed. The simple but inspired answer was provided by Nigel Gresley, who created a corridor in the locomotive's tender that enabled the relief crew to make their way from a reserved compartment through the tender to the cab at the appropriate time (figs. 101–103). Changes of crew took place just north of York, the halfway point of the journey. It is said that Gresley tested out the practicalities of this arrangement by setting out his dining room chairs to the required width to see if he – a large man – could squeeze through the gap.

But there was so much more involved in keeping the non-stop Flying Scotsman moving. The preparation and maintenance of the locomotives needed to be of the highest standards. In 1931 the shed at King's Cross was enlarged and improved with new equipment such as a larger turntable to accommodate the bigger express engines, a travelling crane that could lift locomotives undergoing repair, a water-storage tank that could hold 70,000 gallons and a mechanical coaling plant that could automatically drop 9 tons of coal into the tender of a Flying Scotsman locomotive in just 6 minutes (fig. 109).

Signalling along the route was also improved. The electrification of signals began in the early 1930s as the LNER set about modernising the complex system to ensure that The Flying Scotsman and other expresses could run safely. The large central signalling box opened at King's Cross in 1931 had an all-electric power interlocking frame with 232 levers, 60 long-range colour lights and route indicators. The need to supply the locomotives pulling The Flying Scotsman with the vast quantities of water required for operation was crucial to the success of the non-stop runs. Large water troughs were strategically placed at six points along the east-coast main line, from which the locomotive hauling The Flying Scotsman could scoop upwards of 2,000 gallons of water each time it passed over them. To maintain the troughs teams of men were required to sweep them regularly to prevent clogging, often working while fast expresses sped past on adjoining tracks (figs. 106–108).

Despite the advent of non-stop runs, The Flying Scotsman began to lose its reputation for speed with the arrival of two new streamlined services, The Silver Jubilee (1935) and The Coronation (1937). While The Flying Scotsman could travel between London and Edinburgh in 7 hours, the Coronation could do it in 6, some 2 and a quarter hours quicker than the fastest time at the beginning of the 1930s. However, these new trains – on which an additional supplement was charged – were lighter and had restricted capacity, so The Flying Scotsman remained popular, although it was now advertised as being for 'those who prefer to travel more leisurely'.[1] The introduction of the diesel-pulled Flying Scotsman in 1958 meant that, once again, crews had to change at Newcastle due to the fully enclosed cabs, ending the possibility of regular non-stop runs for the time being. But the concept was still used for publicity events, as in May 1968 when the now-preserved locomotive Flying Scotsman recreated the non-stop run on the 40th anniversary of the inaugural service (see chapter 10), and again in 1991 when BR celebrated the completion of the electrification of the east-coast main line with a record-breaking non-stop run between Edinburgh and London. This journey – a record that remains unbeaten – took just 3 hours and 29 minutes, nearly 5 hours less than the journey took in 1928 and still over half an hour quicker than the fastest scheduled run between the two capitals today, which, rather appropriately, is that of The Flying Scotsman, as run by VTEC.

1   'To Scotland', LNER and LMS advert, *The Times*, 7 July 1938, p.20.

97. The morning rush from King's Cross Station, 1928. Four trains led by A1 Pacific locomotives prepare to depart: from left to right, the 10.15 Leeds Express, the 10.05 Scotch Express, the 10.00 non-stop Flying Scotsman and the 10.20 for Peterborough.

98. LNER A1 Pacific locomotive Flying Scotsman ready for departure with the first non-stop northbound Flying Scotsman service on 1 May 1928.

99. Sir Charles Batho, Lord Mayor of London, with Nigel Gresley, driver Pibworth and William Teasdale, advertising manager for LNER, on the footplate of the locomotive Flying Scotsman before the first non-stop run on 1 May 1928.

100. The first northbound non-stop Flying Scotsman arrives into Edinburgh's Waverley Station, 1 May 1928. The service had been watched by huge crowds along the route and arrived ahead of its scheduled time by 12 minutes.

101. Poster promoting The Flying Scotsman non-stop service, 1928. The poster was designer by Frank Newbould for the LNER and shows the Flying Scotsman locomotive, with the relief fireman and driver just about to take over from their colleagues.

102. The corridor tender on A1 Pacific locomotive Flying Scotsman, 1928. It was the development of this corridor that enabled non-stop running, as crews could change while the train was still in motion.

103. The second driver and fireman relaxing in their reserved compartment prior to going on shift, c.1928.

THE FLYING SCOTSMAN
10·0 A·M· KING'S CROSS TO EDIN

104. Advertisement for the second year of
non-stop running on The Flying Scotsman,
1929. Up to the Second World War the
non-stop summer running of the train
provided a regular publicity boon for
the LNER.

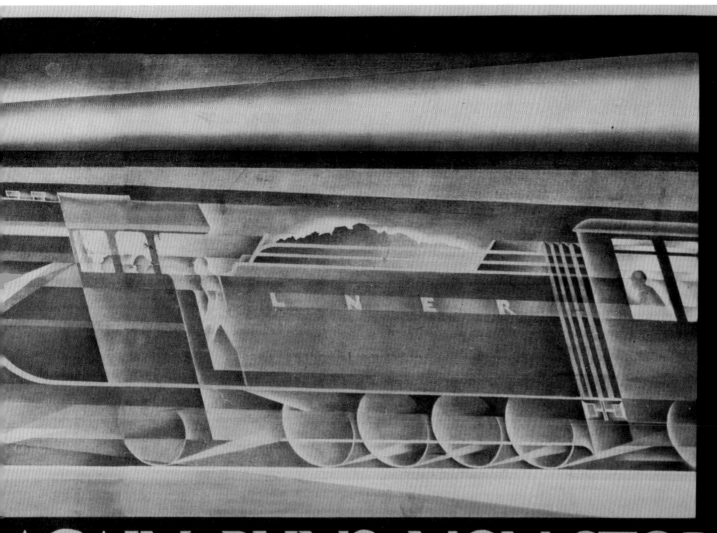

AGAIN RUNS NON-STOP

...IRGH   8TH JULY TO 21ST SEPTEMBER

105. Smoke-deflecting experiment on The Flying Scotsman, King's Cross, 1946. The LNER constantly strove to improve performance and double chimneys were trialled on A3 Pacific locomotive Humorist, which in turn necessitated experiments in smoke deflection to avoid smoke from the new chimneys being blown into the driver's line of sight.

106. LNER publicity photograph entitled 'Assuaging an Expresses's Thirst', showing one of a series of water troughs on the route of The Flying Scotsman, c.1930. Locomotives were fitted with water scoops to enable water to be taken on board as the train passed over each trough at speed.

107. Men cleaning an LNER water trough, *c.*1930. The work was dangerous, with express locomotives running past on adjoining tracks at high speed, but essential, as any leaves and other debris in the trough could compromise the performance of express locomotives.

108. Deltic-hauled Flying Scotsman running through water troughs on the east-coast main line, 1968. The water troughs that lined this and other routes were gradually removed as the Deltic diesel engines replaced steam. The troughs were not immediately redundant, however, as the first Deltics made use of them to scoop up water for steam heating in the carriages.

109. 'Refuelling the Flying Scotsman', LNER poster, 1932. This artwork by Frank Newbould depicts the new coaling plant at King's Cross and proudly announces that the plant can coal The Flying Scotsman in just six minutes. These state-of-the-art coaling plants further demonstrate the LNER's use of innovation to ensure that The Flying Scotsman and its other services remained at the forefront of British railway practice.

110. Men waving from a signal gantry on the east-coast main line at St Albans Road, Hatfield, 16 December 1932. These signals controlled the movements of The Flying Scotsman and all trains from King's Cross Station to the north and were crucial in helping to enable safe and non-stop running of the service.

6. BUILDING THE BRAND

It is one of the ironies of the LNER that, despite the unquestionable success of The Flying Scotsman, the company struggled financially. Its public image as a forward-thinking and successful business helped mask the reality of its reliance on freight for survival, and this was due in no small part to the marketing genius of the company. The LNER was particularly fortunate to employ two brilliant advertising managers, William Teasdale and, from 1928 until 1946, his successor Cecil Dandridge. Both men knew how to build a brand and, crucially, recognised the vital role of advertising (or 'Railway Propaganda' as they called it) in running a modern railway company. Both men were among the most important pioneering ad men that Britain produced. And both recognised the value that could be achieved by raising the profile of the LNER's flagship service, The Flying Scotsman, with the resultant increase in passenger numbers and revenue.

Teasdale was working as the LNER's advertising manager in 1924 when the previously unnamed locomotive 1472 was renumbered 4472 and named Flying Scotsman after the company's most famous train, in time for it to be seen by tens of millions of visitors to the British Empire Exhibition at Wembley. Teasdale was also instrumental in another great publicity opportunity, the trial of a cinema carriage on The Flying Scotsman in 1924 (figs. 126, 127). The LNER also produced a range of Flying Scotsman souvenirs, which served as both a revenue-generating exercise and also extended the visibility of the brand. Customers could purchase a photograph of the eponymous locomotive as exhibited at the British Empire Exhibition, while colour postcards, plates and a cardboard model (fig. 149) were also available. There was also a book about The Flying Scotsman (first published in 1925), the title of which introduced a bold claim: *The Flying Scotsman: The World's Most Famous Train* (figs. 123, 124). The book, costing 1s., contained a history of the route, the locomotives and the rolling stock along with other information related to

the train, and it would go into a further three editions, each reflecting the latest developments in the service. Among the most striking and enduring results of the LNER publicity machine were its posters, particularly those for The Flying Scotsman, many of which utilised the skills of leading artists of the day.

Dandridge succeeded Teasdale in 1928, a year which saw the already high profile of The Flying Scotsman raised further by the publicity surrounding the non-stop runs and luxurious new carriages. Dandridge was a colourful character – he had risen to the rank of Major in the British Army during the First World War and later headed up the Traffic Department of the Archangel Railway in Russia where he served during the Civil War. While in Russia he met a Russian Princess, Olga Galitzin, whom he married in 1924. Under his stewardship, stunts using The Flying Scotsman became a feature of the LNER's publicity. Some of these spectacles involved the train racing planes and speedboats (see chapter 9). Dandridge also arranged for LNER employees to dress in kilts to support Flying Scotsman Week in 1929 and orchestrated a screening of the film *The Flying Scotsman* in 1930 where 'filmgoers' were placed in the queue for tickets carrying a parcel or bag on which Flying Scotsman labels were 'prominently posted'.[1]

Recognising the value of The Flying Scotsman as a brand, Dandridge further extended the range of souvenirs that Teasdale had started. Customers could now buy a Flying Scotsman paperweight (launched in response to the rival LMS producing an ashtray) and an oxidised silver model of the locomotive (fig. 150), both of which were advertised in the national press. But perhaps Dandridge's greatest legacy was the standardisation of lettering across the LNER. This brand identity work was truly innovative and far ahead of its time. Dandridge recognised, before many others, the importance of consistency across the brand and the need to project a clean, crisp and clear image. To this end he employed the well-known artist Eric Gill – a rail enthusiast – to create the LNER's brand identity in 1929. The resulting Gill Sans font was used across the LNER's publicity and advertising material and was formally launched in November 1932 at King's Cross Station, where Gill presented a headboard for The Flying Scotsman with the name of the train painted by the artist himself in the new font (figs. 112, 113). As part of his fee for the work, Gill was later given the opportunity to ride on the footplate of the locomotive pulling The Flying Scotsman; he would later write an amusing account of the journey for the LNER's staff magazine (to which Dandridge contributed a regular column entitled 'Advertising Notes'). At the same time, The Flying Scotsman's own visual identity was developed, being used on materials such as menus and luggage labels.

Iconic posters for The Flying Scotsman continued to be produced, many projecting an ultra-modern image of the service. They included, most famously, a version inspired by the famous Southern Railway poster ('Summer Comes Soonest in the South') showing a young boy looking up at the driver of the train with the words 'Take me by the Flying Scotsman' (fig. 117). Unsuccessful when it was first produced and withdrawn quickly, this poster is now recognised as a classic of the genre. Newspaper adverts for The Flying Scotsman were also common, emphasising the unique qualities of the train, notably its world-record non-stop running and the quality of service on board. Speed was a

key marketing tool in selling the service. One advert selling the attractions of Edinburgh in 1932 encouraged potential tourists: 'See it this year. See it while your eyes are young. The Flying Scotsman will take you. She flies faster to Edinburgh in these days, faster by twenty-five minutes... King's Cross for Scotland.'[2]

Although the nationalisation of the railways in 1948 marked the end of the LNER, it did not diminish the brand or appeal of The Flying Scotsman. C.K. Bird, Chief Regional Officer of the Eastern Division of British Railways, wrote in his foreword to Alan Anderson's 1949 book *The Flying Scotsman*: 'The staff of British Railways regard "The Flying Scotsman" as a rich inheritance from the railways that made it famous, and it will be their aim and privilege worthily to uphold the traditions of the past.'[3] Posters and adverts for the train continued to utilise that 'rich inheritance', and in 1962 BR commemorated the centenary of the train with a re-launched and rebranded service complete with a fibreglass headboard in the form of a golden winged thistle. 'The Wings', as they were known, became the symbol of the service and were used on posters, carriage-window information notices and platform signs. Wings attached to images of the locomotive had been used in advertising posters for The Flying Scotsman as early as the 1920s, and were used once again in marketing for ECT's re-launched Flying Scotsman service of 2011.

1   Cecil Dandridge, 'Advertising Notes', in *London & North Eastern Railway Magazine*, January 1931, p.4.
2   'From a Hotel Window', LNER advert, *The Times*, 10 May 1932, p.12.
3   Alan Anderson, *Famous Train Journeys No.1. The Flying Scotsman*, Brockhampton Press, Leicester, 1949, p.2.

111. LNER brochure produced for the British Empire Exhibition showing the locomotive Flying Scotsman, 1924. Flying Scotsman was one of the star attractions at the exhibition along with Locomotion No.1 (1825), the Great Western Railway's Caerphilly Castle and other notable locomotives.

THE
LONDON AND NORTH EASTERN
RAILWAY COMPANY

Three-Cylinder Superheated
4-6-2 PACIFIC TYPE
Express Tender Locomotive

Exhibited at the
BRITISH EMPIRE EXHIBITION
WEMBLEY
1924

112. The Flying Scotsman locomotive on display at the British Empire Exhibition at Wembley, 1924. The locomotive was prepared to exhibition standard and fitted with embellishments such as brass splashers (above the wheels), making it unique among the A1 class.

113. Artist and typographer Eric Gill affixing his hand-painted Flying Scotsman headboard to the front of A1 Pacific Flying Fox, King's Cross, November 1932. The Gill Sans font adopted by the LNER in 1929 became an integral part of the company's – and The Flying Scotsman's – visual identity.

114. Pages from the Winter 1933 edition of the *Monotype Recorder* showing the LNER's use of Gill Sans typeface, as designed by Eric Gill and issued by Monotype. The pages show the contrast between the old, decorative font used for the LNER brand and the cleaner Gill Sans font.

L.N.E.R. TYPOGRAPHIC (WOOD LETTER) POSTERS **BEFORE** AND **AFTER** THE STANDARDIZATION TO GILL SANS

[*REDUCED LINE BLOCKS*

115. Poster by Léo Marfurt advertising the northbound Flying Scotsman, *c.*1927. The choice of Swiss artist Marfurt for this stylish Art Deco graphic shows how the marketing department at the LNER were keen to keep at the forefront of advertising and design.

116. LNER poster by the Hungarian artist Ladislas Freiwurth for the Flying Scotsman, c.1928. The poster plays on the flying wings device as a representation of a service so well known that no name is needed.

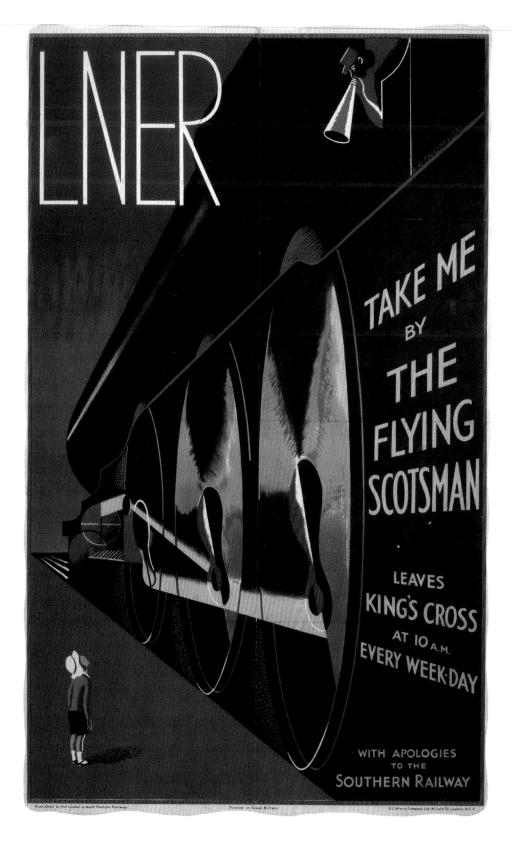

117. 'Take Me by The Flying Scotsman' poster, 1932. This poster depicts the LNER and The Flying Scotsman as the embodiment of speed and modernity, while also having a sly dig at the Southern Railway's similarly posed but more traditionally depicted 'Little Boy' poster. For all its stylish accomplishment, this poster was not well received by the travelling public, and was not re-issued in 1933.

118. 'A Smart Turn Out' LNER poster for The Flying Scotsman, 1935. The poster emphasises the glamorous image of the train with a well-dressed woman holding on to the front of A3 Pacific locomotive Sandwich, named after the winner of the 1931 St Leger horse race.

A SMART TURN OUT

CURTIS MOFFAT

"THE FLYING SCOTSMAN"

LEAVES KING'S CROSS LONDON
AND WAVERLEY STATION EDINBURGH
EVERY WEEKDAY AT 10 A.M.

LONDON & NORTH EASTERN RAILWAY

119. 'The Flying Scotsman' BR poster, 1950. The poster shows an illustration of The Flying Scotsman pulled by Madge Wildfire, one of a new type of A1 Pacific locomotives, with a timetable of services between London King's Cross, Grantham, Newcastle and Edinburgh Waverley.

120. BR poster for The Flying Scotsman, c.1964. By this time the service was being pulled by the Deltic diesel locomotives. The eye-catching, golden, winged-thistle headboard device is a prominent feature of the poster. It is interesting to note that the ladies' retiring room introduced by the LNER in 1928 was still an advertised feature of the service in the 1960s.

BRITISH RAILWAYS

THE FLYING SCOTSMAN

WEEKDAYS

LONDON King's Cross	10.0 am
NEWCASTLE	2.0 pm
EDINBURGH Waverley	4.0 pm
EDINBURGH Waverley	10.0 am
NEWCASTLE	11.58 am
LONDON King's Cross	4.0 pm

Restaurant and buffet cars, ladies' retiring room with attendant
Through carriage from London to Aberdeen, arriving 8.0 pm
Through carriage from Aberdeen to London, departs 6.10 am
Seats reservable from London, Edinburgh or Aberdeen at 2/- each seat

121. LNER luggage label as used on the southbound Flying Scotsman, c.1930. The label depicts one of the A1 or A3 Pacific class of locomotive that had transformed the service in the 1920s.

122. LNER luggage labels for destinations that The Flying Scotsman stopped at or connected to, c.1937. Note that representations of the service now feature the A4 locomotive, the fastest class of steam locomotive in the world.

123, 124. Front covers of the first and fourth editions of *The Flying Scotsman: 'The World's Most Famous Train'*, 1925 and 1931. The two covers show how images of the service projected by the LNER changed over a relatively short time. The locomotive Flying Scotsman on the first-edition cover gives way to the experimental 'Hush Hush' along with a more modern font and style on the fourth-edition cover.

125. The winged-thistle branding seen here at King's Cross Station, *c.*1964. The traditional departure time for the train of 10am remains, but the traditional departure from platform 10 has changed to platform 8.

7. PROJECTING MODERNITY

During the heyday of The Flying Scotsman in the 1920s and 1930s the train was frequently used to trial an array of modern innovations. This can be viewed as an example of how both the LNER and the Scotsman service strove to retain their position as industry leaders, while also reinforcing their public image as leaders of innovation and modernity. The LNER was also – as we have seen – a master of publicity, and knew how to best utilise the attention generated by this use of modern technologies on their trains, particularly the flagship Flying Scotsman service.

The first significant trial of new technology involved the conversion of one of The Flying Scotsman's carriages into a travelling cinema, complete with operator's box and seating for an audience of around 20 (figs. 126, 127). The experience of looking out of the window at the passing landscape gave way to a new sense of escape generated by the moving pictures projected onto a screen at the back of the carriage. As *The Illustrated London News* commented in a report about this development, 'Art is now to compete with nature'.[1] The first cinema-train experiment took place on the 10am departure for Edinburgh from King's Cross on 12 March 1924. It was the first British cinema train, and the film, screened twice on the journey as far as York, was one of the latest Hollywood productions: *Ashes of Vengeance* directed by Frank Lloyd and starring Norma Talmadge, one of the leading actresses of the day. Adverts for the film were displayed on the outside of the carriage, and the blacked-out windows were painted with scenes from the film. The experiment was deemed a success, the *Illustrated London News* noting: 'The pictures were not affected by the oscillation of the train, and the only difficulty was to keep the coach perfectly dark.'[2]

On the same day the southbound Flying Scotsman also included a cinema carriage, in which passengers watched a Hollywood flapper movie starring Corinne Griffith entitled *Black Oxen* or, as the adverts on the side of the train proclaimed, 'The Famous Monkey Gland Film', on account of the story involving an anti-ageing potion. Both films

were silent, and it is not known if any accompanying sound was provided (it seems unlikely given space constraints). Despite attracting considerable publicity, the cinema train experiment was put on hold before reappearing in the 1930s, when the cinema carriage showed a variety of Pathé newsreels. In the 1930s the LNER even employed a uniformed 'cinema attendant' to sell tickets to passengers in their compartments (fig. 128).

In the years leading up to the Second World War other innovations were trialled on board The Flying Scotsman, including television. In 1932 experiments were made by Baird & Co. with the LNER using a 'Baird Televisor' (fig. 131). An aerial was fixed to the carriage roof, and ground connection was made through its wheels and axles. Passengers could hire sterilised headphones for 1s. The experiment attracted considerable publicity, even as far afield as the United States. The LNER was keen to explore uses of technology as a means of improving on-board leisure amenities. Business travellers were also catered for with trials of a dictaphone, which involved dictating into a large speaker positioned on one side of the carriage aisle (fig. 132). This was connected to a set of earphones worn by a secretary sitting on the opposite side of the aisle, who busily typed up the letter on a typewriter.

Wireless broadcasts could also be heard on the train. In 1928 passengers were able to listen to the Derby horse race as broadcast by the BBC. In the same year a world record for train reception was claimed when a group of passengers from Australia travelling to Edinburgh on the train listened to a special programme being broadcast from Melbourne. In the following year the Derby was broadcast once more, and tickets with the result were distributed to those passengers not fortunate enough to be within earshot of the loudspeaker. At 6pm television pictures were then shown of the end of the race and of the winner being led in. Associating the Flying Scotsman service with the speed and glamour of horse racing seems likely to have been quite deliberate. The majority of the A1 and A3 Pacific class locomotives that hauled the train at this time were named after successful racehorses (one was named Trigo after the 1929 Derby winner), and the Derby broadcast became a tradition on the train until the Second World War. In addition to receiving radio, broadcasts were also made from The Flying Scotsman. In 1925 a broadcast was aired from the train, by means of a portable transmitter positioned on the locomotive's footplate.

The LNER also experimented with playing music via radio. This led to The Flying Scotsman having what the rail historian Christian Wolmar has called 'the world's first mobile DJ'.[3] The question of the suitability of music in trains was questioned by *The Times* in January 1930: 'Whether the traveller wants this added luxury is another question. Already there is far too much music provided for unsuitable occasions, and the railways will be unwise to give up one of their remaining advantages – reasonable privacy and quiet in travel.'[4] The common complaint of passengers today concerning noise on trains is clearly not new. *The Times* did see some merit in the experiment if it were possible 'to reserve a single coach for the transmission of news and music on very long journeys. Earphones fitted to each chair would be a better method of distributing the sounds than through loudspeakers.'[5] The LNER seemed to take this advice, and for the price of 1*s.* passengers could hire GEC Radio headphones from the on-board uniformed 'Radio Boys' who served on The Flying Scotsman and other wireless-enabled express trains (figs. 138, 139).

Musical broadcasts on The Flying Scotsman were not to last, due to the large licence fees demanded by the Performing Rights Society. The LNER had invested heavily in wireless equipment and disputed the claim (made in 1933) by arguing that as passengers had tuned in using headphones no public performance had taken place. A court ruling went against them, however, and musical broadcasts ceased, although the traditional Derby broadcast continued, fully supported by the BBC; on the same day in 1936 passengers listened to the race after tuning in to hear coverage of the maiden voyage of the transatlantic liner RMS *Queen Mary* (fig. 140).

Interest in The Flying Scotsman as a subject for radio and television programmes has always been strong. A decade after the first broadcast was made from the train in 1925, driver Taylor, one of the regular Scotsman drivers, featured on the BBC radio programme 'Railway Rhythm' alongside fellow drivers on other elite British expresses. In 1952 the legendary BBC broadcaster Richard Dimbleby fronted a documentary on the Night Scotsman, and in the same year the BBC's first female news reporter Audrey Russell interviewed The Flying Scotsman's driver on radio (figs. 134, 135). The train had become associated with radio, television and cinema in some quite unexpected ways, and it would even – as we shall see in the next chapter – go on to become a movie star itself.

1 'The "Flying Scotsman" as a Cinema: The First Film in a Train',
   Illustrated London News, 22 March 1924, p.497.
2 Ibid.
3 Christian Wolmar, *Fire & Steam*, London 2007, p.247.
4 'Music in Trains', *The Times*, 30 January 1930, p.12.
5 Ibid.

Opposite
126. Interior of the cinema-train carriage, 1924. Newspaper reviews of the innovation were favourable, but it was noted that there was difficulty in keeping the carriage perfectly dark.

127. Britain's first 'Cinema Train' being trialled on The Flying Scotsman, King's Cross, 1924. The first film shown was *Ashes of Vengeance* (1923) starring Norma Talmadge, which was shown twice in abridged form between London and York.

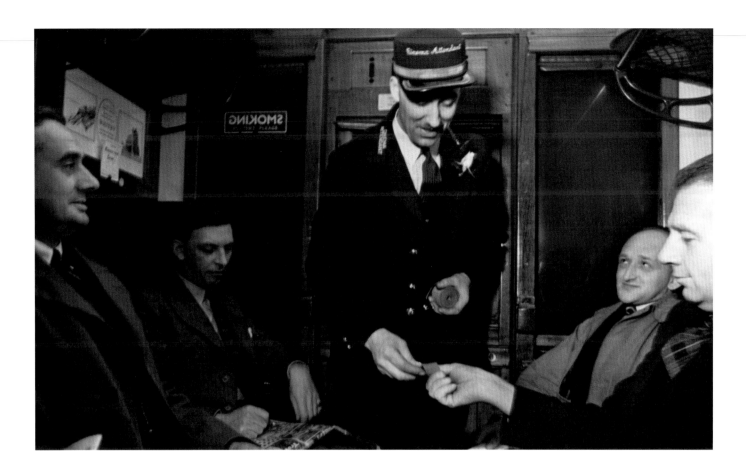

Above
128. Cinema attendant selling tickets on board an LNER express, c.1936. Although the use of cinema carriages showing feature films on The Flying Scotsman was short lived, the trial did lead to the appearance of cinema trains showing Pathé newsreels on other services.

Left
129. Films set up at the back of an LNER cinema carriage, c.1936. For the price of 1s. passengers could watch a variety of newsreels.

Right
130. Interior of an LNER cinema carriage, c.1936. Lessons having been learnt from the 1924 trials, later cinema carriages were purposely designed to block out all daylight, and proper cinema-style seating was also now provided.

Below
131. The Baird Televisor being demonstrated on an LNER express, 1932. Three years earlier passengers on The Flying Scotsman had been able to see recorded television pictures of the end of the Derby horse race.

Left

132. Dictaphone demonstration on an LNER express, *c.*1928. The Dictaphone, as an aid to conducting business on the train, was trialled on The Flying Scotsman and other services.

Below

133. Set photograph of filming for 'The Night Scot Prepares', King's Cross shed, 1952. Peppercorn A1 locomotive Borderer is being prepared to pull The Night Scotsman in front of BBC television cameras filming a Richard Dimbleby documentary about the train. The programme was broadcast on 29 August 1952.

Above
134. Richard Dimbleby inspects The Night Scotsman's locomotive during filming of his BBC documentary about the train. The film showed preparations being made to the train and included interviews by Dimbleby with 'backroom boys who keep the railways going', among them Mr Simpson, Superintendent of Motive Power at King's Cross, who is shown here.

Right
135. The BBC's first female news reporter Audrey Russell interviewing driver Dicksee on the footplate of A4 Pacific locomotive Sir Nigel Gresley at the head of The Flying Scotsman, 13 October 1952.

136. Interior of an LNER experimental radio-broadcasting coach with Leslie McMichael of McMichael Radio, July 1924. This was an early LNER experiment in radio organised with the Radio Society of Great Britain. Radio became a popular attraction on The Flying Scotsman, and passengers were eager to tune into broadcasts of the Derby, royal weddings and other national occasions.

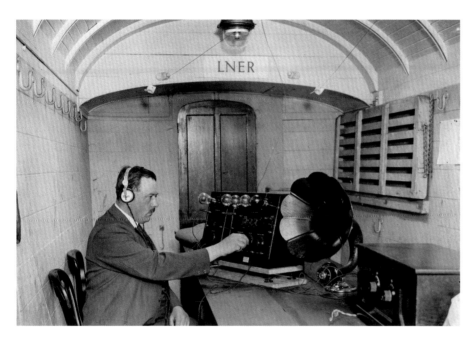

Above right
137. Equipping an LNER brake third-class carriage with an aerial, *c.*1930. By the time this photograph was taken three carriages had already been fitted with receiving apparatus, including two fitted with radio gramophones.

Left
138. A 'Radio Boy' leaning out of an LNER carriage window, *c.*1930. The young men employed in this role were each provided with a special uniform with the word 'Wireless' on the cap.

Opposite
139. A 'Radio Boy' hiring out headphones to passengers on an LNER express train, *c.*1930. The headphones, made by GEC, were sterilised and cost 1s. to hire.

140. Passengers on board The Flying Scotsman listening to radio broadcasts on 27 May 1936. The radio broadcasts on this day comprised commentary on the maiden voyage of RMS *Queen Mary* followed by live commentary of the Derby horse race.

8. POPULAR CULTURE

In February 1892 *The Strand Magazine*, a hugely popular monthly magazine, featured one of Arthur Conan Doyle's most celebrated Holmes escapades, 'The Adventure of the Speckled Band'. The publication enjoyed a massive circulation – approximately 500,000 at its height – due in no small measure to readers' interest in the latest adventures of the detective Sherlock Holmes. But in the same edition readers could also enjoy a different type of adventure – an account of travelling on the footplate of the most famous train in Victoria's Empire. F.G. Kitton's 'A Night Ride on the "Flying Scotchman"' is an exciting account of a ride on one of GNR's Stirling Single locomotives on the Grantham-to-King's Cross leg of the southbound Flying Scotsman service in October 1891. Kitton explained his choice: 'this Scotch Express (significantly called "The Flying Scotchman") is believed to be the fastest train in the world'.[1] Readers of *The Strand* may have been familiar with the exploits of Holmes and Watson, but Kitton now drew them into the adventures of another duo in the form of Collarbone and Watson, that is to say Harry and Samuel, respectively fireman and driver of The Flying Scotsman, another icon of Victorian popular culture.

Such was the popularity and reputation of The Flying Scotsman that as early as the 1880s it gave its name to the popular 'Flying Scotchman' pen, which, its makers boasted, could 'glide like an express-train'.[2] By this time the train was also the subject of numerous coloured postcards and would later become the focus of jigsaws, models and cigarette cards too – all part of the highly developed marketing operation to publicise the brand (see chapter 6). At the height of The Flying Scotsman's fame in the 1920s and 1930s there was no shortage of souvenirs relating to both the train and the locomotive that the enthusiast could purchase. In 1925, to mark the 100th anniversary of the Stockton & Darlington Railway, a black-and-white cut-out cardboard model of the Flying Scotsman locomotive was produced. Following the success of the non-stop service, which began in 1928, further products were released, including a Flying Scotsman desk weight, cigarette lighter and biscuit tin. At the same time, the national press carried adverts for a 'Scale Model finished in oxidised silver of the famous "Flying Scotsman" Locomotive which daily performs the world's record non-stop run King's Cross to Edinburgh'.[3] These could be purchased for the price of 2*s*. 6*d*., with free delivery, from the LNER's offices across the country, or from station bookstalls (fig. 151). In 1927 Hornby produced their first Flying Scotsman model railway set, which has been a staple product for the firm ever since and enjoyed by many generations (fig. 150).

From 1937 younger children could read about the adventures of the Scotsman locomotive in Doris Crockford's popular illustrated book *The Flying Scotsman* (figs. 157, 158). In the story the locomotive decides to go on an adventure to the end of the east-coast railway track, but, unable to go beyond John O'Groats, the engine, missing its driver and fireman, starts to fear that it will rust away. Needless to say the ending is a happy one. It is interesting to note that Doris Crockford is also the name of a character in J.K. Rowling's *Harry Potter* books, which are themselves noted for a named express train that departs King's Cross from a set platform at a set time. The illustrations in Crockford's book show the locomotive with a face in place of its smokebox some eight years before the publication of an iconic series of books that used the same device: the Revd W. Awdry's 'Railway Series' featuring Thomas the Tank Engine. Awdry would in fact later include the Flying Scotsman locomotive in his work, in a 1968 story which also featured the Scotsman's fictional sister locomotive Gordon, the express engine.

References to The Flying Scotsman and its eponymous locomotive were also made in other branches of the arts. George Scott-Wood, known as the pioneer of swing music in Britain, composed a *Flying Scotsman* piece, which was later popularised further by the BBC orchestra conductor, band leader and 'Wurlitzer King' Sidney Torch (fig. 160). Yet it was in the cinema that The Flying Scotsman found its most successful route into popular imagination. The film credited as being the first British 'talkie' in 1929 was *The Flying Scotsman* (figs. 9, 153–55). Featuring stars of the day Moore Marriott, Pauline Johnson and, in his screen debut, Ray Milland, it is a tale of love, adventure and villainy aboard The Flying Scotsman and the locomotive of the same name. Directed by Castleton Knight, the film was shown in cinemas across the country, wowing audiences with astonishing stunts performed by the cast themselves, including Pauline Johnson having to scramble along the outside of the train while it was travelling at around 70mph. Johnson performed this stunt herself, while wearing high heels and a fur coat. Nigel Gresley was said to have been unimpressed, and a statement emphasising that the film in no way showed the actual practice of the LNER was inserted into the end credits.

This film seems to have made a particular impression on one young film director named Alfred Hitchcock. The Flying Scotsman plays a central role in Hitchcock's classic 1935 movie *The 39 Steps* (fig. 156). It is aboard The Flying Scotsman (hauled by A3 Pacific locomotive Trigo) that Richard Hannay (played by Robert Donat) makes his getaway from London, performing his famous escape as the northern section of the train crosses the Forth Bridge. Hitchcock appears to have gone to great lengths to faithfully represent the train; at one point in the film Hannay, being chased by the police, runs through the Scotsman's Louis XVI-style restaurant, which was an accurately reproduced stage set, and there is also use of genuine footage of the train at both King's Cross and Edinburgh Waverley. The Scotsman has made many other appearances in film and television over the years. It is tempting to speculate whether the train taken by Jack Carter (played by Michael Caine), heading north to Newcastle to avenge his brother's death at the beginning of Mike Hodges's cult 1971 movie *Get Carter*, is The Flying Scotsman. Things had run full circle, and the train that had first shown passengers films in its innovative cinema carriage had become part of the movie scene itself.

1 F. G. Kitton, 'A Night Ride on the Flying Scotchman', *The Strand Magazine*, Volume III, number 14, February 1892, pp.195–201.
2 Advert for Macniven and Cameron's pens, *Illustrated London News*, 5 April 1884.
3 'Flying Scotsman', LNER advert, *The Times*, 11 September 1928, p.16.

Opposite
141, 142. Postcards showing The Flying Scotsman in the 1890s. The first shows the train with a Stirling Single at its head at King's Cross, and the second shows the train pulled by an Ivatt Atlantic in full flight. Such postcards document the early popularity of the train.

King's Cross Station, G.N.R.

G.N.R. "Flying Scotsman"

THE FLYING SCOTSMAN
L.N.E.R.

THE FLYING SCOTSMAN

CHURCHMAN'S CIGARETTES.

"THE FLYING SCOTSMAN."

143–146. Cigarette and tea cards depicting The Flying Scotsman, 1920s and 1930s. The cards show the changing guises of the train at this period with its various locomotives and rolling stock .

147. Postcard depicting the Flying Scotsman locomotive and also representing the train, c.1928. In this photograph the locomotive can be seen with its corridor tender, which allowed for changes of crews on long-distance non-stop runs.

"FLYING SCOTSMAN," L.N.E.R., 4472.   4-6-2.   3-CYLINDER ENGINE.   TYPE A.1.

ONE OF THE WORLD'S MOST POPULAR ENGINES, AND USED FOR THE FAMOUS LONDON TO ABERDEEN RUN.

GAUGE OF TRACK	4 FT. 8½ INS.	FIRE BOX WIDTH		7 FT. 9 INS.
CYLINDERS	20 INS. x 26 INS.	TUBES	NUMBER 168, DIAMETER 2¼ INS.	
DRIVING WHEEL DIAMETER	6 FT. 8 INS.		32	5¼ INS.
BOILER INSIDE DIAMETER	6 FT. 3 5/8 INS.	8-WHEELED CORRIDOR TENDER.		
PRESSURE	180 LBS.	CAPACITY · WATER		5000 GALLONS
FIRE BOX LENGTH	9 FT. 5½ INS.	COAL		9 TONS

148. Postcard from Pitlochry, Scotland showing The Flying Scotsman, c.1930. This was part of a series of postcards depicting the train that were sold from popular holiday destinations such as Pitlochry, even though the train itself did not serve many of these places.

Expressing My Views of   PITLOCHRY

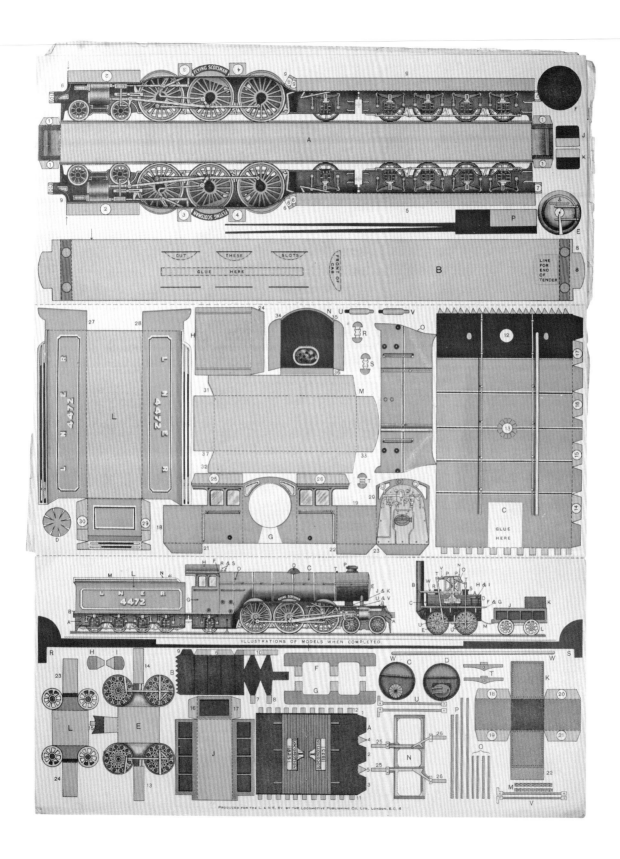

Opposite
149. Cardboard cut-out model of the Flying Scotsman locomotive as sold at the British Empire Exhibition at Wembley in 1924 and 1925. On one Saturday alone it was reported that 400 of these models were sold.

Right
150. The Flying Scotsman clockwork train set by Hornby, *c.*1927. The Flying Scotsman has endured to this day as one of Hornby's most popular train sets.

Above
151. Souvenir oxidised-silver model of the locomotive Flying Scotsman sold by the LNER from 1928 onwards. The exceptionally successful model sold for 2s. 6d. as far afield as Australia and New Zealand.

Right
152. *Daily Herald* photograph from the Model Railway Club Exhibition in Central Hall, Westminster, April 1935. The large LNER-owned model of the Flying Scotsman locomotive proved a popular exhibit.

Left
153. Still from the film *The Flying Scotsman* directed by Castleton Knight, 1929. At the heart of the film was the country's most famous train and the locomotive of the same name.

Below
154. Still from *The Flying Scotsman*, 1929. Credited as the first British 'talkie', the film helped cement the fame of The Flying Scotsman train. The film also marked the screen debut of the celebrated matinee idol Ray Milland (centre).

Above
155. Still from *The Flying Scotsman*, 1929. This scene shows the heroine played by Pauline Johnson scrambling across the outside of the train while it travelled at around 70mph. Johnson did these stunts herself dressed in a fur coat and high heels and reportedly collapsed after completing this scene, but went on to do it again after the first take was spoiled.

Right
156. Still from Alfred Hitchcock's *The 39 Steps*, 1935. This scene shows Richard Hannay (played by Robert Donat) in a third-class compartment of The Flying Scotsman escaping from the scene of a murder he did not commit. This image shows the train at Edinburgh Waverley where Hannay realises that he is a wanted man when he spots a newspaper article about himself. He re-joins the train and soon after makes a famous escape on the Forth Bridge.

157, 158. Front cover and illustration from Doris Crockford's children's book *The Flying Scotsman*, published by Oxford University Press, 1937. The illustrations by Rachel Boger and Henry Cartwright show the locomotive with a human face, just as the Revd W. Awdry's railway stories featuring Thomas the Tank Engine would when they were published several years later.

Above

159. 'The Flying Scotsman' Spitfire, 1941. During the Second World War industry was encouraged to sponsor new aircraft, and this Spitfire was paid for by the LNER and its employees. Tragically, it crashed in the Brecon Beacons during an operational exercise in November 1941 killing its pilot Flight Sergeant Charles Colborne Gardner. A later Spitfire paid for by the LNER also took The Flying Scotsman name.

Right

160. Score for 'The Flying Scotsman' piano music by George Scott-Wood, published in 1950. Scott-Wood was a hugely popular musician and band leader who had worked with notable figures such as Gracie Fields, Max Miller and Ivor Novello. He recorded 'The Flying Scotsman' with his accordion band in 1950, and the music was later popularised further when recorded by Sidney Torch, the well-known BBC broadcaster and pre-eminent cinema organist of his day.

9. TRAINS, BOATS AND PLANES

Just as the LNER were keen to publicise their adoption of the latest technical innovations in order to project an image of The Flying Scotsman as the train at the forefront of invention, so they also sought to exploit its reputation for speed. On 30 November 1934 – St Andrew's Day – the locomotive Flying Scotsman, driven by William Sparshatt while running high-speed test trains between London and Leeds, became the first steam locomotive to achieve an authenticated speed of 100mph (fig. 171). Although it was the locomotive rather than the train that achieved this record, it still helped to further associate the words 'Flying Scotsman' with speed. This reputation had developed from its earliest days in the 1860s and was solidified with the high-speed 'Races to the North' between rival railway companies in the 1880s and 1890s. To ensure that the train remained in the media spotlight in the 1920s and 1930s a series of stunts that played on this reputation for speed were staged involving the train, a variety of planes and even a speedboat.

The first major stunt was performed in 1928, the year in which the profile of The Flying Scotsman had already risen due to the introduction of non-stop runs. On 15 June a race was arranged between the 'Down' or Edinburgh-bound Flying Scotsman and an Imperial Airways Armstrong-Whitworth aircraft of the latest design, named 'City of Glasgow' (fig. 161). Train and plane each left from their respective departure points – King's Cross Station and Croydon Aerodrome – at the traditional Flying Scotsman departure time of 10am. The winner would be the first crew to arrive at Edinburgh's Waverley Station; the aircrew were to land at Turnhouse Aerodrome, the airport for Edinburgh, where waiting motor cars would be ready to whisk them to the station. The train would run non-stop, but the plane made two stops to refuel at Bircham Newton in Norfolk and Cramlington in Northumberland.

Before the departure a breakfast had been held at the Savoy Hotel where the two parties met to hear Air Vice Marshal Sir Arthur Vyell Vivian read out letters from Sir Eric Geddes and Sir Ralph Wedgwood, the chairmen of the airline and the railway company respectively. Sir Ralph's letter expressed his hope that 'this comparison of the speed of the train and air travel might lead the public to appreciate the great strides which were being made in the convenience afforded for long distance travel both by rail and air services'.[1]

Both companies fully played up the sense of occasion. The plane was piloted by Captain Gordon P. Olley, a First World War fighter ace, who would go on to become the first pilot to fly a million miles. Among his passengers was Inspector Birkett who, at 79 years of age, was the oldest driver employed by the LNER and was making his first flight. The reserve pilot, Captain G.P. Jones, travelled on the train.

On several occasions during the race the plane had to double back to allow the train to catch up. This did not please Birkett who, *The Times* noted, complained 'that "this circling back business" was making a fool of the train'.[2] This doubling back also resulted, rather comically, in the plane following the wrong train for a while. This was understood only when the train that the plane was following, which was in fact The Junior Scotsman, crossed the Royal Border Bridge at Berwick and the planned signal of a flashlight from the fourth carriage of the train was not forthcoming. Realising the mistake, Olley turned the plane towards Edinburgh at speed but encountered heavy rain and further delays, and although the plane did eventually make contact with The Flying Scotsman it was too late. The train, headed by A3 Pacific Sansovino (named after the 1924 Derby winner), arrived victorious into Waverley Station.

Captain Olley was gracious in defeat and wrote about the momentous journey in an amusing article for the LNER staff magazine, recounting how he had been refreshed by the LNER's hospitality in Edinburgh and 'returned to King's Cross in an excellent sleeping berth, glad to think the day had been a success'. Reflecting on his error, he finished his article by recommending 'that you paint big white letters on the roof of the real non-stop "Flying Scotsman" to prevent further mistakes by airmen in the future'.[3] This is exactly what the LNER did when, three years later, they hosted another spectacle involving train and plane (figs. 162–165).

The stunt held on 20 May 1932 was not strictly speaking a race but rather a test for a Marconi radio being trialled on both plane and train. An aerial was fixed onto the roof of one of The Flying Scotsman's carriages, and radio equipment was set up in the brake van, while 'Flying Scotsman' was painted in large letters on the roof of the rear carriage to ensure correct identification. Passengers on the train were able to communicate with passengers on the 42-seat Imperial Airways 'Heracles' plane flying above them. Other LNER publicity stunts carried out during the 1930s pitted The Flying Scotsman against boats. In 1931 a speed boat raced various trains, including The Flying Scotsman, and the occasion was captured for posterity in a series of photographs and a Pathé newsreel (figs. 166–168). The contest of 'Speed Boat v. Flying Scotsman' (as the Pathé newsreel proclaimed) involved the celebrated motorboat racer J.W. Shillan racing LNER expresses on a two-mile stretch of the River Ouse near Huntingdon, which runs parallel to the east-coast main line. In one race, won by The Flying Scotsman, the boat and train were also joined by an aeroplane piloted by Captain Geoffrey de Havilland, the celebrated aircraft designer and pilot.

Never a company to overlook the publicity value of stunts involving The Flying Scotsman, the LNER also staged photo opportunities at King's Cross where the 'fastest' men of the day could be photographed shaking hands. Thus at the launch of the summer non-stop Flying Scotsman service in 1932, driver William Sparshatt (at this point yet to drive the record-breaking 100mph run) was photographed leaning out of the cab of the Flying Scotsman locomotive with the world's fastest man, Sir Malcolm Campbell. In the following year Sparshatt – again at the controls of the Flying Scotsman locomotive – shook hands for the media with Captain Geoffrey de Havilland who had just won the prestigious London-to-Scotland air race, the King's Cup. Such events solidified the reputation of The Flying Scotsman and its locomotive as icons of speed.

1   'To Scotland by Rail and Air', *The Times*, 16 June 1928, p.7.
2   Ibid.
3   Gordon P. Olly, 'Spotting the "Flying Scotsman"', *London & North Eastern Railway Magazine*, vol. XVIII, 1928, p.338.

161. The Flying Scotsman prepares to race an Imperial Airways plane, King's Cross, 15 June 1928. This photograph is not in fact authentic and has been doctored for publicity purposes; the plane actually took off from Croydon Aerodrome. The train, pulled by A1 Pacific Sansovino, eventually won the race after the pilot of the plane lost sight of The Flying Scotsman and started following the wrong train by mistake.

Above
162. The words 'Flying Scotsman' being painted on the roof of one of the train's carriages, 1932. This was done to help a pilot keep track of the train during a Marconi radio test, in which passengers on the train communicated with passengers on a plane.

Left
163. Imperial Airways aeroplane Heracles and The Flying Scotsman pulled by A3 Pacific Grand Parade during the Marconi radio test run, near Newark, 20 May 1932.

164. Marconi radio telegraphy transmitting and receiving apparatus in the brake van on The Flying Scotsman for the test with the Imperial Airways plane. The call signal used for the train was 'G5FL'.

Below

165. Aerial view showing The Flying Scotsman racing through the countryside on the day of the Marconi Radio test in May 1932. Just visible at the rear of the train are the words 'Flying Scotsman' painted in large white letters to prevent the plane following the wrong train as had happened during the plane-versus-train race in 1928.

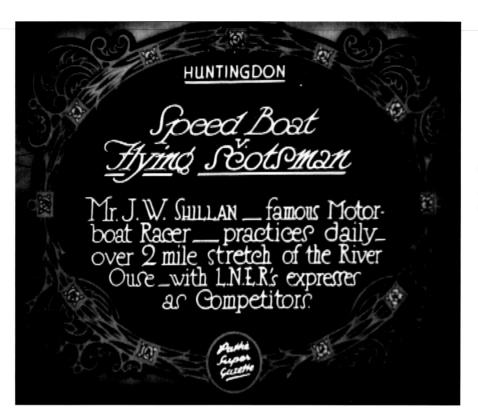

166. Still from British Pathé newsreel 'Speed Boat v. Flying Scotsman'. The film shows the races between the speedboat racer J.W. Shillan and various LNER expresses, including The Flying Scotsman, on the River Ouse near Huntingdon in 1931.

167. J.W. Shillan in his speed boat racing the 'Up' Flying Scotsman in 1931. The locomotive is A1 Pacific Donovan.

168. J.W. Shillan's speedboat and The Flying Scotsman racing a plane piloted by Geoffrey de Havilland, 1931. The train, running at around 80mph, won this particular race along a stretch of the River Ouse.

Left

169. Sir Malcolm Campbell wishing 'A Fast Run', King's Cross, 1932. Here Campbell, the world's fastest man, is shown passing on his wishes to driver Sparshatt prior to the departure of The Flying Scotsman. The locomotive is Flying Scotsman itself, and Sir Nigel Gresley, Chief Mechanical Engineer, is also in the photograph (standing, left).

Below

170. Captain Geoffrey de Havilland shaking hands with driver Sparshatt and fireman Smith of The Flying Scotsman, 1933. Celebrated aircraft designer de Havilland had recently won the King's Cup, the prestigious London-to-Scotland air race.

Opposite

171. Driver Sparshatt with fireman Webster in front of LNER A1 Pacific Flying Scotsman, 1934. This photograph was probably taken at King's Cross Station on the day Flying Scotsman became the first steam locomotive to officially achieve a speed of 100mph.

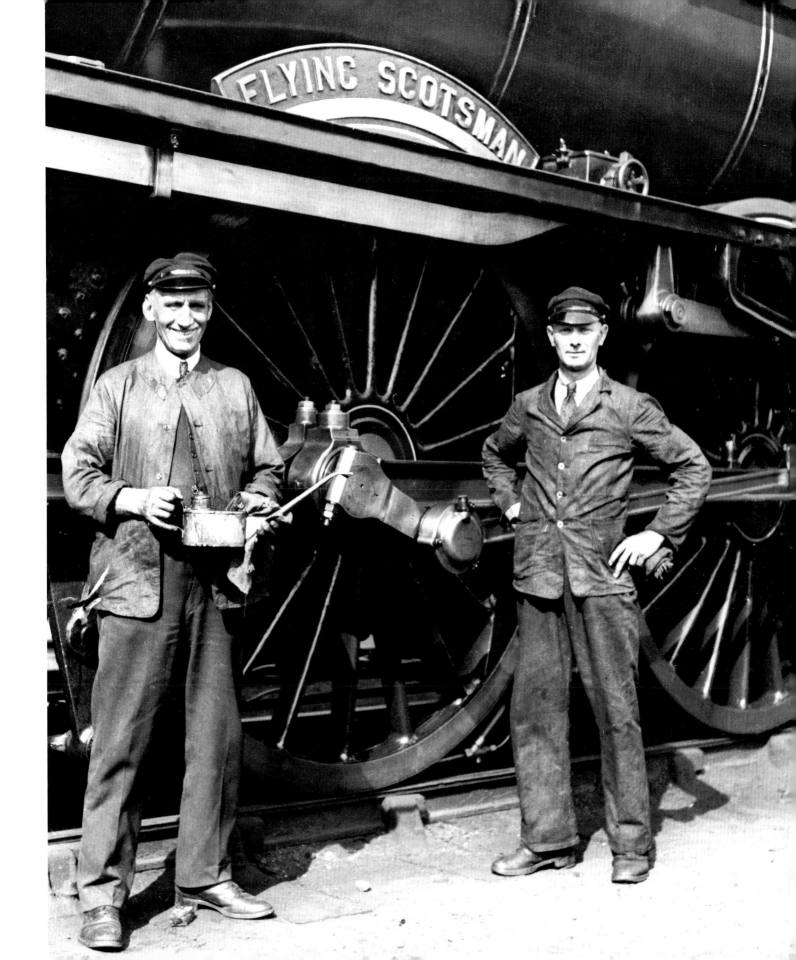

10. MODERNITY AND NOSTALGIA

In 1968 the British Government gave official backing to a ground-breaking new railway development. After years of delay, BR was finally given the go ahead to develop the Advanced Passenger Train (APT), a train conceived for running at speeds of up to 155mph and one that could take the numerous curves on Britain's Victorian railways – including the east-coast route of The Flying Scotsman – at high speed by tilting.

The technology was revolutionary. Sections of the media, notably *The Times*, were enthusiastic. Other countries, particularly the United States, watched with interest. In 1968 BR was on the verge of leading the world in high-speed rail development. Yet the general public seemed more interested in lamenting the passing of the steam age than acknowledging these technological advances. British popular culture at this time was reflective of this national mood. The great poet and champion of railway heritage John Betjeman wrote and narrated a documentary 'Railways For Ever!' inspired by the last BR steam-pulled service, while the rock band The Kinks lamented its passing in their song 'The Last of the Steam Powered Trains'.

This wistful mood was captured by a BBC documentary broadcast on 11 August 1968, the day main-line steam officially ended on BR. The documentary ends with the camera silently sweeping through the scrapyard at Barry, south Wales, past hundreds of redundant steam locomotives awaiting the cutters' torch. The film had celebrated the 'sole survivor' of main-line steam, the locomotive 4472, Flying Scotsman. While The Flying Scotsman train continued to adapt, as it always had, to the latest technological advances, the Flying Scotsman locomotive had become a symbol of nostalgia for a passing age, and its fame began to outstrip that of the train it had once pulled. To discover how this happened we must look back some five years to a bitterly cold winter's day at London's King's Cross Station.

On 14 January 1963 Britain was in the grip of 'The Great Freeze', which saw London buried under two feet of snow. The cold weather did not deter the huge crowds who descended on King's Cross Station to witness the final departure in active service of Flying Scotsman (fig. 176). The locomotive had been saved from obscurity by Alan Pegler, a flamboyant businessman and former pilot. Pegler went on to restore the locomotive to something approximating its classic LNER image. Gone were the double chimney and smoke deflectors added by BR in the early 1960s. Gone too was its BR number, 60103, and colour, replaced with the LNER apple-green livery and her historic number, 4472. The locomotive toured the country in its newly preserved guise and became, once again, a media darling. In 1966, during an episode of the BBC's hugely popular children's programme *Blue Peter*, presenter John Noakes announced to millions of watching children that he was standing in front of 'Flying Scotsman, the most-famous steam locomotive in the world!'

The enthusiasm of Pegler and Noakes helped to solidify the status of the Flying Scotsman locomotive, and for the first time its fame exceeded that of the train of the same name. If the 1920s had been the decade of 'The World's Most Famous Train' then the 1960s was the decade of 'The World's Most Famous Locomotive'. So when the locomotive attempted to run non-stop from London to Edinburgh on 1 May 1968, to mark the 40th anniversary of the first non-stop run, the BBC were on hand to record the event, and the resulting documentary was broadcast to mark the passing of the age of steam on Britain's railways.

But The Flying Scotsman also played its part in this event. Pulled by a Deltic diesel, the train departed King's Cross alongside the Flying Scotsman locomotive at the traditional departure time of 10am (fig. 179). With Flying Scotsman services old and new departing together, this photo opportunity led to extensive press coverage. This was not the first time that there had been a staging of Scotsmans old and new. To mark the launch of the new Flying Scotsman train service in 1938, the locomotive Stirling Single No.1 was brought out of retirement to haul a recreation of the

1888 Flying Scotsman train, which ran alongside the latest train, hauled by A4 Pacific Sir Nigel Gresley (fig. 178).

Indeed, it was one such staging that had prompted Alan Pegler to rescue the Flying Scotsman locomotive. In June 1962, to mark the centenary of The Flying Scotsman train, the locomotive had been lined up beside the Deltic-pulled present-day Scotsman service at King's Cross. However, a BR manager ordered the steam locomotive to be banished from view as, in his opinion, it jarred with the modern image that the organisation was trying to project. Pegler witnessed this incident, prompting him to become involved in the preservation of the locomotive. It was to be the beginning of a new chapter for the locomotive which, in addition to raising its profile in the United Kingdom, also saw it travel to countries including the United States and Australia, and become the first locomotive to circumnavigate the globe. Following a national fundraising campaign the locomotive was acquired by the National Railway Museum in York in 2004, after its last private owner, Tony Marchington, had put it up for sale.

Although the decline of The Flying Scotsman's profile continued under BR, the name enjoyed a revival in the era of rail privatisation, when GNER, who held the route franchise from 1996 to 2007, embossed each carriage of their trains on the east-coast route with a heraldic device and the words 'Route of the Flying Scotsman'. In 2011 the service was once again re-launched by then operator ECT as a one-way service only, departing Edinburgh for London at 5.40am each weekday. To commemorate the re-launch a Class 91 locomotive, 91101, was re-liveried with the name 'Flying Scotsman' on the sides and a winged-thistle device on the front end (fig. 50).

At the time of writing, The Flying Scotsman is the fastest train service connecting Edinburgh and London. There are still simultaneous departures from Waverley and King's Cross stations at 10am, although these are not officially named 'The Flying Scotsman'. When the Stagecoach/Virgin consortium took over the east-coast route franchise in March 2015 a poster proudly proclaimed that they were 'Still flying the Scotsman'. Although its fame is far from the heyday of the 1920s and 1930s, the future of The Flying Scotsman service looks secure for some time yet.

172. 'Then and Now' LNER poster, 1930. The LNER played on the history of the service and regularly placed old next to new in their marketing materials to emphasise the modernity of the current train, as in this poster by A.R. Thomson.

173. 'The Flying Scotsman' BR poster, 1962. The artwork shows old and new locomotives that had pulled the train: an early locomotive designed by Archibald Sturrock and the latest Deltic diesel.

174. A3 class 4-6-2 locomotive Flying Scotsman with a passenger train emerging from Welwyn North Tunnel, Hertfordshire, 1959. The tunnel is daubed in graffiti protesting against the use of the new Deltic diesel locomotives, which were about to supplant the steam-powered A3s on services such as The Flying Scotsman.

175. Poster announcing a campaign to save the Flying Scotsman locomotive, 1962. The locomotive was due to be scrapped, and the campaign to save it represented an acceleration in the railway preservation movement. The Flying Scotsman became symbolic of the passing of a way of life, the final representative of the steam age.

176. A3 Pacific Flying Scotsman at King's Cross, 14 January 1963. The iconic locomotive prepares for its last run in active service. The locomotive is pulling the 1.10pm service to Leeds but will be uncoupled from the train at her Doncaster birthplace to undergo restoration work to return it to the original LNER number and colours.

Above
177. Flying Scotsman GNR locomotives old and new, 1922. The latest locomotive type to haul the train, Nigel Gresley's A1 Pacific Sir Frederick Banbury, is lined up alongside one of the earliest, Patrick Stirling's Single No.1.

Left
178. The Flying Scotsman trains old and new at Stevenage, 1938. To mark the launch of an all-new Flying Scotsman train in 1938, the LNER recreated the train from 50 years earlier, the date of the first of the Railway Races to the North. The 1888 train is pulled by Stirling Single No.1 and the 1938 train by A4 Pacific Sir Nigel Gresley.

179. The Flying Scotsman trains old and new at King's Cross, 1 May 1968. The Flying Scotsman locomotive recreated the first non-stop run of The Flying Scotsman on the 40th anniversary of that date. Here the steam-powered train leaves King's Cross alongside its modern Deltic-hauled equivalent.

180. Old and new Flying Scotsman motive power, York, 2005. The locomotive Flying Scotsman is seen with a GNER HST, one of its successors on The Flying Scotsman service.

181, 182. Stills from British Pathé newsreel 'Extra! Flying Scotsman Leaves For USA!', 1969. The Flying Scotsman locomotive left Liverpool for a North American tour, taking in more than 2,200 miles of American railroad track and cities such as Boston, Dallas and Washington. This first tour, part of an official British trade mission, was a great success, but the second leg from Texas to Toronto in 1970 ended in financial disaster for Alan Pegler and saw the locomotive impounded. Flying Scotsman finally returned to the United Kingdom under the ownership of Sir William McAlpine in 1973.

Opposite
183. Poster advertising a run in the train pulled by the Flying Scotsman locomotive in Australia, 1988. Interestingly, the artwork depicts the locomotive with The Flying Scotsman train headboard. During her Australian trip Flying Scotsman broke the world record for the longest non-stop run by a steam locomotive, running 422 miles without stopping.

Overleaf
184. The Flying Scotsman locomotive undergoing restoration work, 2015 at Riley & Son Ltd in Bury, Greater Manchester. An extensive overhaul of the locomotive had ensured its continued survival for generations to come.

FLYING SCOTSMAN

 Melbourne 9th July — 6th August **P&O** Containers

QANTAS

STEAMRAIL VICTORIA

is proud to support the visit of THE FLYING SCOTSMAN to Australia

STEAMRAIL VICTORIA
restores and operates
"THE VINTAGE TRAIN" ®

*Bring the Family and join us
on one of our monthly
Vintage Train excursions.*

Phone: 629 4806

*Available for Charter for your
Group Excursion, Social Club
Outing or Company Promotion.*

Phone: 397 2439

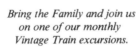

STEAMRAIL VICTORIA, P.O. Box 61, Caulfield East. 3145

FURTHER READING

There are a vast number of publications covering aspects of the Flying Scotsman story. Much use has been made by the author of contemporary newspaper and magazine accounts, notably the archives of *The Times* and *Illustrated London News* as well as railway periodicals, particularly *The Railway Magazine* and the *London & North Eastern Railway Magazine*, copies of which can be publicly accessed via the National Railway Museum's library and archive centre, Search Engine. The BBC's 1968 documentary *4472-Flying Scotsman* was also very useful (accessed in June 2015 via BBC iPlayer).

The following is a selection of publications that have also been used in putting this book together:

Allen, Cecil J., *Famous Trains*, Liverpool, 1928.
Allen, Cecil J., *The Gresley Pacifics of the L.N.E.R.*, London, 1950.
Allen, Cecil J., *Titled Trains of Great Britain*, 1st edn, London, 1946.
Anderson, Alan, *Famous Train Journeys No.1 The Flying Scotsman*, Leicester, 1949.
Anon., *The Flying Scotsman: The World's Most Famous Train*, 1st edn, LNER, London, 1925.
Anon., *The Flying Scotsman: The World's Most Famous Express with the World's Longest Daily Non-stop Run*, 3rd edn, LNER, London, 1929.
Anon., *The Flying Scotsman: The World's Most Famous Express with the World's Longest Daily Non-stop Run*, 4th edn, 1931.
Baldwin, James S., *The Flying Scotsman Story*, Stroud, 2014.
Brown, F. A. S., *Nigel Gresley: Locomotive Engineer*, London, 1962.
Ellis, Cuthbert Hamilton, *The Flying Scotsman 1862–1962: Portrait of a Train*, London, 1962.
Grinling, Charles H., *The History of the Great Northern Railway 1845–1902*, London, 1903.
Gwynne, Bob, *The Flying Scotsman: The Train, the Locomotive, the Legend*, Oxford, 2010.
Hughes, Geoffrey, *Flying Scotsman – The People's Engine*, York, 2005.
Hutcherson, Margaret, *Let No Wheels Turn: The Wrecking of The Flying Scotsman, 1926*, Washington, Tyne & Wear, 2006.
Kitton, F. G., 'A Night Ride on the Flying Scotchman', *The Strand Magazine*, vol. III, no. 19, February 1892, pp. 195–201.
Nock, O. S., *The Great Northern Railway*, London, 1958.
Pegler, Alan et al., *Flying Scotsman*, 2nd (enlarged) edn, London, 1970.
Roden, Andrew, *Flying Scotsman: The Extraordinary Story of the World's Most Famous Train*, London, 2007.
Wolmar, Christian, *Fire & Steam*, London, 2007.

PICTURE CREDITS

This book has been produced as part of the National Railway Museum's Flying Scotsman season, delivered in partnership with